The Miracle of Sons

The Miracle of Sons

Celebrating the Boys in Our Lives

Jamie C. Miller and
Jennifer Basye Sander

A Perigee Book

A Perigee Book
Published by The Berkley Publishing Group
A division of Penguin Putnam Inc.
375 Hudson Street
New York, New York 10014

Copyright © 2003 by Jamie C. Miller and Jennifer Basye Sander
Text design by Tiffany Kukec
Cover design by Ben Gibson
Cover photo by Lambert / Getty Images, adapted by Ben Gibson

First edition: February 2003

Visit our website at www.penguinputnam.com

Library of Congress Cataloging-in-Publication Data

Miller, Jamie C.
The miracle of sons : celebrating the boys in our lives / Jamie C. Miller and Jennifer Basye Sander.
p. cm.
ISBN 0-399-52851-2
1. Boys. 2. Child rearing. I. Sander, Jennifer Basye, 1958– II. Title.

HQ775 .M655 2003
649'.132—dc21
2002035515

Printed in the United States of America

10 9 8 7 6 5 4 3 2 1

CONTENTS

Acknowledgments ix

Foreword · *Tina Cole* xi

Introduction xvii

PART ONE

Gifts of the Heart

Kodak Moments · *Ana Veciana-Suarez* 3

The Winning Pitch · *Linda Horsley Cook* 6

Going on a Joy Ride · *Janet Konttinen* 10

The Big Question · *Rosemary Roberts* 13

The Shelf · *Sandra Burt* 17

Batman Kisses · *Michael T. Powers* 21

PART TWO

Defining Moments

The Red Bike · *Barbara Workinger* 27

Stretch Marks · *Sara Camilli* 35

Eyes to See · *Rebecca R. Howell* 39

Hearing Evan's Voice · *Ann Reuthling* 42

The Disguise · *Sharon Brody* 45

A New Form of Praise · *Lissa Lee*   48

The Lesson of the Lightning Bugs · *Michael T. Powers*   52

PART THREE

Pink and Blue

The Balancing Act · *Cheryl Erwin*   57

Super Bowl Challenged · *Karin Kasdin*   61

The Sperm Versus the Egg · *Sarah Harrison*   67

The Doll · *Amy Oscar*   72

Snakes and Snails · *Candy Chand*   76

Of Whiskers and Cowlicks · *Melanie J. Grimes*   79

PART FOUR

Blessings

Puppy Love · *Ron Brand*   85

Our Little Piece of Heaven · *Teri Brinsley*   90

A Very Special Christmas Stocking · *Anne Frazier*   95

Lunch Money Miracle · *Linda Doty*   98

Sleep with Your Angels · *Jaymie Reeber Kosa*   102

The Horse with No Name · *Kathryn A. Beres*   106

Daily Bread · *Teri Brinsley*   109

PART FIVE

Obstacles

Great Expectations · *Rosemarie Riley*   115

When Moms Are All Wet · *Janet Konttinen*   121

Karate Lessons · *Lisa Mangini*   124

Teacher on the Mound · *Linda Watts*   129

Golden Rules · *Bev Grasso*   132

Baby Mine · *Lynne Marie Rominger*   135

PART SIX
Ties That Bind

Exchange of Gifts · *Elaine Reiser Alder*   143

Stuffed Angel · *Rosemary Roberts*   149

Lucky Number 13 · *Julie Larson*   154

The Overcoat · *Sara Camilli*   157

Inseparable · *Julie Elsberry*   161

Rites of Passage · *Denise Roy*   165

PART SEVEN
The Journey

My Superman · *Linda Dobson*   173

The Maze · *Jamie Miller*   177

The Summer I Almost Lost My Golf Partner · *Bob Dreizler*   182

He'll Turn Out Okay If You'll Let Him · *Lisa Lehr Dodd*   186

I Hope She Says "Yes" · *Pamela R. Blaine*   192

Overdue · *M. J. Kornfeld*   196

Room with a View · *Penny Warner*   199

ACKNOWLEDGMENTS

Our warmest thanks and deepest gratitude to the talented people at Perigee Books, especially our dedicated editor, Sheila Curry Oakes, and her assistant, Terri Hennessy. We are also thankful to our agent, Sheree Bykofsky, for making this book a reality, and to our personal assistant, Candy Brand.

No book is complete without the contributions of others, and we wish to thank the many mothers and fathers of boys who so generously shared their inspiring stories with us. We'd also like to thank our families for their love and devotion, and especially our sons—Jonathan, Julian, Alex, Ian, Seth, and Ryan—for giving us six good reasons to write about the joy of raising boys.

FOREWORD

If nothing else, we remember the logo. Those three pair of gangly legs, cartoon-skinny, misshapen, shooting down into three pair of oversized and equally misshapen loafers and tennis shoes. The words seemed a bit dignified against the backdrop of bony ankles and rolled-up pant legs, which, if you zoomed in closer, were certain to expose bruises, cuts, scrapes, and mud caked onto hairy calves. But two things were certain, simply by the way those feet shot out in random directions: one, these were the feet and legs of *boys,* and two, these boys—like all boys—were ready for action and headed for mischief.

But there it was anyway, boldly and proudly announcing to television audiences everywhere: *My Three Sons,* as if the "owner" of this trio of boys was either actually proud of the fact—or resigned to it.

In 1967, after seven years of being an all-male TV show, the producers had decided it was time to introduce—*gasp!*—a girl. And so I was introduced on the set as "Katie," Robbie's girlfriend and soon-to-be-wife and soon-after-that-to-be-mother of . . . yes, all-boy triplets. Before I came on the scene, Fred MacMurray as Steve Douglas was the widowed father of three sons and had been doing a fine job raising his boys . . . with the help of crusty but capable Uncle Charley, that is. Yes, they had their challenges, but the growing pains of this unconventional family made life in the Douglas household delightfully unpredictable, and *My Three Sons* was to become one of television's longest-running sitcoms.

For five years, this was my TV family—"Dad," Robbie, Chip, Ernie, Uncle Charley, and three growing baby boys (they actually used two sets of twins in the beginning so there'd be an extra look-alike baby to rotate in, should one become sick or excessively cranky).

I had to adapt quickly to this all-male family that was so used to doing all-male things. My character was to remain girlish and vulnerable but feisty and spunky at the same time. In other words, I had to hold my own in a vast sea of testosterone, which, at times, required the strength of Solomon and the patience of Job. At the end of each day at the studio, I'd come home to two more boys—a husband and a son, born just a few months before I started *My Three Sons*. Looking back on those years, I guess it was a good thing I liked boys!

So why did this show have one of the longest runs in Hollywood? Most family comedies in those days were centered on strictly nuclear families—*I Love Lucy, Father Knows Best, Leave It to Beaver, The Donna Reed Show*—two-parent households and their biological offspring. *My Three Sons* initiated what was to become a popular trend in television—that of a widowed parent raising a family. A whole slew of similar shows like *Family Affair* and *Full House* followed, all about families who survived and even thrived without any maternal influence, and although not a totally realistic notion, it got the audience's sympathy and made for humorous sitcom material.

Part of the show's uniqueness was its new definition of family, but the real strength of *My Three Sons*, I believe, was the fact that, at its core, it was about boys. The one universal truth about the world of boys is this: It is *never* boring. Those buzzing, boisterous, naughty creatures dash and dart through our lives with more pep than the Energizer bunny. Boys can turn an ordinary afternoon at the park into a Steven Spielberg action/adventure movie—props, sound effects, and all. And when they've completely worn us out or made us wonder if they'll ever get past the punching-kicking-wrestling-drumming-disrupting "stage," they turn around smiling, say something that thoroughly melts our hearts, and make us forget we were ever annoyed by their messes or mischief in the first place.

What I learned on *My Three Sons* was later confirmed as I raised my own two sons—there is an endearing simplicity and naiveté about boys that make them irresistibly lovable—sometimes, in spite of themselves. You always know where you are with boys; admittedly, it's not always a pretty place, but still, you know. Erma Bombeck reminds us, as only she can:

With boys you always know where you stand. Right in the path of a hurricane. It's all there. The fruit flies hovering over their waste can, the hamster trying to escape to cleaner air, the bedrooms decorated in Early Bus Station Restroom.

But the reflections in this book reveal a deeper side to the story. They convince us that a growing boy is a more complex creature than we might've thought, but that each boy, in his own way, needs to be understood, appreciated, and loved.

I remember well the three distinct personalities of Robbie,

Chip, and Ernie on *My Three Sons*, and how their father tried to understand and nurture each of them. Those were scripted relationships, where happy endings were just a matter of typing in the right responses and series of events. Typical of most sitcoms of the day, each episode of *My Three Sons* was tied up neatly by the end with an unmistakable moral to the story, usually taught by "Dad"—the ultimate voice of reason. In fact, after each script was written, I remember Fred MacMurray and Fred DeCordova (the producer) sitting for long hours, analyzing whether or not the episode conveyed enough "principle," and then making changes and adding lines until they were satisfied sufficient lessons had been taught. Indeed, by the end of each show, Fred MacMurray's commonsense solutions to almost any problem made him seem like a practically perfect dad.

Perfect parenting exists only on TV. In the real world, there is certainly no unified or elegant theory for raising three sons—or even one. The pat answers we get from Hollywood are rarely as simple as they look, the theories from parenting experts are usually thrown out after the first try, and we find ourselves, mostly, going from the gut and parenting from the heart. And occasionally—if we're lucky—we get it right.

In this book, you'll meet mothers and fathers of sons who juggle and experiment and sacrifice their way through parent-hood—sometimes succeeding, sometimes failing—but who manage to face their challenges with faith, courage, and a sense of humor. The job of parenting is never over. We keep our fingers crossed for our sons and worry about them well into adult-hood, and no matter how old they get, they still remain our *boys*.

The triplets I "raised" on TV are almost thirty-five years old now (I was a *very* young mother), and probably have sons of their own. I think I'll track them down and see if they remember *anything* I taught them!

—Tina Cole
"Katie" on *My Three Sons*

INTRODUCTION

Miracle? Sons? What miracle? What can we be talking about? In today's world, no one in their right mind would equate the two words, at least after following the news in any given week. During the past decade, the words *sons* or *boys* have much more often been associated with things like low self-esteem, ADHD, drugs, aggression, alcohol, anger, and violence. But not *miracle*.

The world tells us our boys are in trouble—and it's not just teenage boys, either. The experts warn that more boys than girls will die as infants, be diagnosed with learning disabilities in the early grades, be sent to the principal's office in middle grades, be suspended from high school, and eventually commit more crimes than girls.

We, as parents of boys, listen and are concerned. We, as a nation, watch and are frightened. What has gone wrong here? What is to become of these bad boys?

We look at our baby boys asleep in their cribs and think there could be nothing more beautiful. Is it even remotely possible that this precious bundle—our own little miracle—could someday do something mean or dishonest or violent? Will he grow up to be sullen, rude, or emotionally illiterate, as the experts caution? It seems so unlikely, but we begin to question our competence as parents, because after the frightening stories in the news and the talk-show attention to the subject, raising a son to become a responsible adult in today's world suddenly seems like such a crapshoot.

But this negative and frightening definition of today's boys doesn't fit *your* little darling—your adorable curly-haired toddler who makes you laugh uncontrollably with his baby talk and smothers you with wet kisses day and night. Or your smart-as-a-whip eight-year-old who scored in soccer last week, practices the piano, and even makes his bed once in a while. This isn't *your* sixteen-year-old who just got his first job at the local music store, loves to go hiking, and recently asked a girl to the prom by presenting her with a long-stemmed red rose. No, these reports of depressed, oppressed, emotionally detached demons are not referring to *your* sons.

Or *ours*. Like many of you, we are the parents of boys (six sons between us), and most of the time we actually like them. No, they're not perfect—not by a long shot—and yes, they smell and make messes and weird noises, but all of that pales compared to the exuberance and fun they bring to life. Perhaps it's time that parents are reminded and reassured that most boys, despite the media's focus, grow up to be quite well-adjusted teenagers and, much to everyone's surprise, turn out just fine. They've even been known to cause their parents incredible joy along the way.

So with this in mind, we started talking to other parents of boys and found many mothers, fathers, and grandparents who, like us, actually enjoyed raising their sons. We found good boys all over the country—caring, intelligent, sensitive, and funny boys—all at various points along the path to becoming exceptional young men. The heartwarming true stories that follow will help you as parents keep your sense of humor and perspective about what's normal and what simply comes with the territory in raising sons. By reading about the experiences of parents who have been there—and survived—you'll gain new insight into the world of boys and their various life passages.

You'll read about defining moments with boys—like the story of a mother who helps her young son triumph over a lifelong speech impediment; a father who finds the link to his relationship with his teenage son on the golf course; a twelve-year-old boy who becomes the town hero when he sacrifices winning a baseball game to help a friend; and a mother who finally sees the fruits of her parenting labors as she accompanies her young son on a snowy-day paper route.

These are not pie-in-the-sky accounts of perfect boys from perfect homes. No, you'll read about families with challenges to overcome, lessons to learn, and sometimes pain and tragedy to deal with. But woven throughout is the hopeful and comforting message that we're all in this together and that we can grow wiser from our shared experiences. A message, too, that perhaps we need to lighten up a little and simply enjoy our boys as they energetically romp through our lives.

It has been said that, "after the work comes the miracle." We know all too well that raising a son—or any child—is work. And work certainly has its rewards. But it is only when we view the work of raising a boy as a true labor of love, that we will find the miracle.

—Jamie Miller and Jennifer Basye Sander

"A boy is a piece of existence quite separate from all things else and deserves a separate chapter in the natural history of man."

—*Henry Ward Beecher*

PART ONE

Gifts of the Heart

"In boyhood I have had more delight on a haymow with two companions and a big dog—delight that came nearer intoxication—than I have ever had in all the subsequent holidays of my life."

—John Burroughs

Kodak Moments

Ana Veciana-Suarez

WE ARE PLAYING HOOKY, Ben and I. Well, he is, at least. It's a school day, a day of spelling tests and social studies projects. But instead of fidgeting in a classroom, he is headed north in the family car.

Ben is eight years old, the fourth of five children, and he often complains he doesn't get enough of my attention. I worry that he might be right, because I am forever juggling work and household duties. So I have chosen him to accompany me on this business trip in hopes of righting past wrongs. I envision shared secrets and heartfelt revelations, two days full of Kodak moments.

Soon after we have paid our first toll, I try to strike up a conversation. He is not interested. Instead, he takes the G.I. Joes from his backpack and places them strategically on the door handle, against an armrest, and between seats. In my rearview mirror, I catch glimpses of my little boy at work, converting the backseat, which he hardly ever has to himself, into a battlefield.

I am determined to make the most of our time together, so I try again, hoping for an exchange that will lead, with a little coaxing, to bonding. I get nowhere and begin to fret. Are my attempts too little, too late? Then I remind myself that children—my children, at least—do not open up like a padlock with a key. They talk when they want to, and sometimes not at all.

So I leave him to his play and turn on the radio. Near mealtime, I give him the option of choosing any restaurant he wants, hoping our first dinner alone together will be in a fancy restaurant with real cutlery and a tablecloth—something special. He spots a fast-food joint instead. Grudgingly, I order chicken for me and burger and fries for him.

Things aren't turning out as I had planned, but before disappointment can settle in, he tells me about something that happened in school. I counter with an anecdote about work. That leads to a story about food fights in tennis camp and another about teammates who can't make weight in football.

Then, just like that, the conversation is over. I'm still hungry, but not for food.

Finally, we arrive at the hotel. It is a grandiose structure of marble floors, indoor trees, a goldfish pond, and boutiques. We ride up the glass elevator, staring down. Then: Wow! Our room is a suite. He bolts for the phone. "You should see this place," he tells the family back home. "It's half a football field!"

I am still hoping for that Kodak moment, a fuzzy, sepia-toned communion of mother and son. But no sooner have I opened my mouth to begin a meaningful, soul-baring conversation than he sprints around the room, plops down on an overstuffed chair, and deposits his feet on the coffee table. He is content to watch TV as if I weren't there.

Later, after a day of what I consider missed connections, I tuck him in and he snuggles close to me. I read him my presentation. Then, he opens his book; I thumb through mine. Just as he is about to fall asleep, he mumbles, "Hey, thanks, Mom."

It suddenly occurs to me that this short trip is a metaphor for the way we parent: We give our children what we think they need, and they take what we offer and make it their own. Maybe this was all the attention he wanted from me, nothing more, nothing less.

I kiss his cowlick and turn off the light. I know many wrongs have been righted—for this night, at least.

The Winning Pitch

Linda Horsley Cook

THE WORN WOODEN BLEACHERS at the ball-park were hot and splintery. I took a seat on the front row among the sparse but devoted fans who had shown up for the baseball game on this scorching summer day.

I watched as my son, Ryan, wound up and pitched the ball. I heard the crisp slap of leather against leather as the ball hit the catcher's mitt. "Strike!" yelled the umpire. I saw a flicker of a smile quickly cross Ryan's face before he regained his look of deep concentration. This was serious business to my twelve-year-old son. As the "new kid in town," he just couldn't miss this chance to gain some respect.

A fly buzzed around my head. I waved it away as the ball slapped into the catcher's mitt again. "Strike two!" Ryan's teammates cheered him on. This could be their second out, and they were anxious to get up to bat again.

"Strike three!" yelled the umpire. Ryan's team was jubilant.

Then Joey came out of the dugout. Joey had been born with Down's syndrome. As he picked up the bat and walked over to home plate, I watched Ryan carefully while Joey loosened up with a couple awkward practice swings. I was the only person besides Ryan who understood the dilemma Ryan faced as Joey stood there to bat.

I vividly remembered the day we had met Joey. I had agreed to baby-sit him on the days his mother was at work. On the first day, Joey walked in, marched straight over to Ryan, and held out his hand. With confidence, poise, and a bit of childlike innocence, he said, "Hi, I'm Joey. What's your name?"

After he introduced himself to Ryan, he talked to each of my other children. His easy nature and friendly personality soon put us at ease.

Later, when I was doing dishes, Joey walked into the kitchen and stood in front of a chore chart with the names of my children on it. He read off each name without any help. It seemed to me that through the help of his family, Joey had achieved a great deal in his thirteen years. Instantly, I admired his parents.

We quickly discovered that Joey was an avid baseball player. In fact, he brought his glove and cap that very first day. From then on, Ryan worked with Joey and showed him how to hold the bat and how to swing properly. They practiced for hours to perfect Joey's ability to hit the ball. If Ryan threw the ball slowly enough, Joey could hit it almost every time.

Then one day, Joey announced that his baseball team would be playing Ryan's team the very next game. Ryan pulled out his schedule, and sure enough, Joey was right. He told Ryan over and over again that he could hardly wait because he had never had a hit in a game before, and he knew he could hit the ball if Ryan was the pitcher.

Ryan had come to me quietly later that day and wondered what he should do. He wanted Joey to succeed by finally getting a hit in a game. But he also felt an obligation to his team to pitch his best. Ryan knew Joey could never hit one of his fast pitches. Quite a dilemma for a young boy—a sobering dilemma even for an adult. I told Ryan that it was a difficult decision, but one he would have to make on his own. I had tried to teach him kindness and compassion throughout his life, and now it was time for him to search his own mind and heart for answers.

Now that moment of decision had arrived. Ryan stood on the pitcher's mound facing Joey. He turned and looked at his teammates. They knew Joey was an easy out—in fact, the third out. But they were suddenly quiet. Ryan looked at his coach, who nodded back his encouragement. Then he quickly glanced up at me. Hesitatingly, Ryan took off his hat, wiped the sweat from his forehead, and gazed intently at Joey. He took the ball in hand, wound up, and then gently lobbed the ball, carefully and slowly, just as they had practiced for weeks. Joey swung—and then, crack! It was a hit!

Joey was so shocked he just stood there looking at the ball. Suddenly everyone, including the boys on the opposite team—Ryan's team—started yelling, "Run, Joey!" For a few moments, a boy's dream of hitting a ball became more important than an easy out.

Joey finally came out of shock and ran. By the time he safely made it to first base, the whole ballpark was standing and cheering. The first baseman was jumping up and down with excitement. Several boys ran over and gave Joey a congratulatory pat on the back and high fives, and the smile on his face could only be matched by the smile on Ryan's. The respect Ryan sought from his peers had come in a very unexpected way. He had learned that afternoon that there was more than one way to win.

Going on a Joy Ride

Janet Konttinen

ONE EVENING, A mother from school called and said that the next day was her little boy's birthday. They were celebrating out of town the following week, but for his actual birthday he begged to have my three daughters spend the afternoon at his house. He said they were the "funnest" friends he'd ever had. On one hand, I wasn't surprised, since my girls were enthusiastic playmates who could hold their own with boys, but on the other, I worried that this is how the triplet party-girls featured in *Playboy* magazine got started.

With the girls gone, it would be one of the rare times I'd have alone with my son. To make the most of it, I suggested we stay home and clean the refrigerator. But he'd just learned how to ride his two-wheeler and asked if we could go for a bike ride on a real bike path instead. I offered the compromise of splitting our time between housework and a short bike ride. Because he'd seen the meat drawer, he insisted we ride bikes first.

I loaded the bikes onto the bike rack behind the car and found two bottles of water and a helmet for my son. I knew I should wear a helmet, too, but chose to risk cerebral injury rather than appear at the grocery store later with "hat head."

After we parked, I took down my son's little bike and noticed I'd incorrectly put mine on the car and the front wheel had gotten bent. I knew I had less than four hours to figure out how it was all my husband's fault. We started down a beautiful bike path along the San Francisco Bay. It was cool and sunny, and I followed behind my son while I struggled to keep control of my wobbly wheel. He had challenges of his own and periodically made unexpected turns across the whole path and into the plants. He'd just lift his feet up above the brush and stammer "Whoa!" until he could maneuver himself back. Then we'd both laugh. I thought about how much I loved his spirit.

As we careened along, a bicycler zoomed up behind us and said quietly, "On your left." That meant we needed to do our best to scoot over to the right so he could pass. Eventually, we saw an elderly gentleman with a walker way up ahead. My son asked, "Can I say the thing about being on the left?" "Sure," I replied. My son started yelling, "Hey, look out! We're on your left. You better move over, we're almost there! Watch out!" Without even looking, the man went straight for the safety of the bushes and seemed surprised that instead of a huge group of racing bikes ready to mow him down, it was just the two of us.

It was low tide, and my son suggested we stop and walk down on the beach to search for artifacts left behind by pirates. Sure enough, we found one of their old mayonnaise jars. We also found a stranded jellyfish, and I congratulated my son on finding the best piece of sea glass. I knew all the work was piling up at home—laundry, bill paying, the meat drawer—but the chores could wait. We were scaring old people and stashing putrid crab pinchers into our pockets.

We continued our ride until it was time to turn around and head back to pick up my daughters. My son thought we deserved a drink from our water bottles, so we sat on a wooden bench overlooking the bay and tasted each other's. Mine was plain, and we agreed that his carbonated one tasted better. We talked about lizards and swimming, and unlike everybody we knew, we thought the movie *Antz* was better than *A Bug's Life*. A breeze kicked up and like so many times before, I reached over and swept my hand across his forehead, pushing his sandy brown hair back into place. He said I could have all of his water I wanted. We climbed back on our bikes and laughed about a funny story a lady recently told us about her dog.

We liked how the sunshine felt on our backs, my friend and I.

The Big Question

Rosemary Roberts

I'LL NEVER FORGET THE exact moment in time when it hit me—that the four-year-old boy quietly gazing out the window of my pickup, my son, Sean, was the embodiment of a profound, old soul . . . one who could simply reach out and touch the heart of humankind with a philosophy far beyond his years. In that moment, I knew, single mother and all, I had been blessed with a special child for which my very best had to be given every day, every moment, and with every breath . . . beyond what we tell ourselves at the start of parenthood, and with all the honesty I could muster. God, I knew, had big plans for him, and despite any hardship that came my way, I was the one chosen to guide and nurture him.

It was an otherwise typical evening, one of those "dark by 4 o'clock" winter nights. I had picked Sean up from the sitter and was navigating the rain-soaked freeway amidst a sea of commuters who, like myself, wanted to get home and call it a day. It sounds a little goofy, but I loved drive time with Sean. It was great catch-up time, sort of the precursor to lengthy table talk over dinner. Sean and I often had deep conversations during our commutes, like the time he informed me that our friend Greg didn't need to hunt deer for food. He could eat chicken, hamburger, or fish. Furthermore, he could go to McDonald's, Mr. T's, or even Choo-Choo's, our favorite breakfast joint. He didn't need to hunt deer, legal or not. He wasn't an Indian . . . he had choices.

Needless to say, any old answers of pacification to Sean's questions on life (a bad habit we adults often indulge with our children), or the assumption that worldly topics were beyond his understanding was a route that proved not only disrespectful, but even more so, futile. He asked straight-up questions and expected straight-up answers from me. He thought things through on his own and always had a rational, logical explanation for his opinions, and he could articulate them well. Such wisdom might be expected from a twelve- or fifteen-year-old, but it was a challenge I was unprepared for at this age. Dubbed by another preschooler's mom as a three-foot attorney, Sean was an observant boy, and his views on the world, of which he was fascinated by and eager to understand, were to be respected. On this night, he would turn his selfless and tender view of the world up a notch. With a sigh of seriousness, he spoke through the darkness.

"You know what makes me really sad, Mom?" he asked.

My stomach dropped as I was instantly sent into a deep sea of fear, frozen in the moment as the possibilities ran warp speed through my mind. Was the statement I had dreaded for two years now about to hit home; how his little heart longed to be back in the same house with his father, together, the three of us? That he worried about his dad being lonely? Maybe he was sad about Kassie, our Australian shepherd who got out the gate and never came home—another victim of the divorce when I left and couldn't take her to our new home. Divorce, two homes, separate schedules, a runaway dog . . . was it all too much? "Be brave and just face the problem head-on," I told myself. "You knew there would be difficult bridges to cross and worries to quail. Be an adult! Be brave. Be honest."

Brave, my rear. I've probably screwed him up forever with my selfish desire for happiness and passion in my world. So what if my marriage wasn't fulfilling, tender, or reassuring? What would I say if this was "it": that moment he wanted an explanation?

"What?" I forced out, striving to maintain calm and stay in my lane on the freeway, avoiding those little bumps that say, "Hey lady! The game's right here! Eyes on the road and attention forward please!" Then I waited, holding my breath while my hands gripped the wheel and my eyes focused intently on the road ahead. "Bring it on, Seanster," I thought. "Whatever it is I'll deal with it." With that, Sean enlightened me.

"It makes me really sad when old people lose on *The Price Is Right*. It's nice when the young people win, too, but they have their whole lives to work and save up for all that stuff . . . old people don't have that much longer. I just think it's better when they win."

With that off his chest, Sean turned his attention back outside the window. As I loosened my grip on the wheel and felt the blood begin to flow into my fingers again, I said a silent thank-you to God . . . several, actually. Thank you for making me strong enough to do what I thought was best during times of great uncertainty. Thank you for helping me be brave, honest, and diligent in my duties as a mom. And most of all, thank you for not letting me underestimate the heart, thoughts, and spirit of the little guy you sent me. If this is any sign of what's to come, I can hardly wait.

As I reached over to stroke Sean's cheek, all the while holding back a proud tear, he flashed his trademark casual, "connected to all that's right in the world" smile.

"You Sean," I said, ". . . think a lot for such a short guy. Have I told you how much I love you today?"

The Shelf

Sandra Burt

ERIC HAD DRAWN THE toughest spot in the family. Half the time, he was in trouble for fighting with one or the other of his brothers. The middle of three boys, he had on either side of him fellows who were nothing like him at all. The oldest and the youngest were both intense, studious, and intellectual and were most content alone in their rooms, reading, playing quiet games, or categorizing their latest collections—of rocks, coins, stamps, or whatever took their fancy.

Eric liked to collect, too, but he chose creative, offbeat items. I was happy to donate to his current stash of buttons—a large, bright mélange of shiny, sparkling, and interesting shapes, often found spread out all over his bed. Mostly, though, Eric like to play—loud, energetic games— like tag, tree-climbing, or a tackle version of any game that required a ball or stick. He had always been very strong, so roughhousing with either brother had brought about actual injuries on more than one occasion—and anger on the part of his parents.

What Eric wanted most was to have people around him who liked his kind of exuberant play, and he was constantly disappointed that neither of his brothers wanted to join him. In frustration, he would often burst into their rooms, hoping that the excitement (or more often, annoyance) of the intrusion would garner him some companionship. This behavior frequently provoked fights. I spent a lot of time feeling that what I really needed was training as a referee.

Then came a big change in Eric's life: a new baby brother, Archie. From the beginning, Archie was different—he liked Eric's loud, exciting presence and looked forward to his return from school each day. When he was old enough to run around, he squealed with joy when Eric bounded in and announced, "Chasing time!" The two would tear around the house until they collapsed in giggles. My husband and I were relieved that Eric and Archie had found each other; there was a new kind of peace in the commotion of our home.

When Eric turned eleven, he decided to attend a summer camp that seemed tailor-made for him. It was a creative arts camp, offering experiences from photography to woodworking, animal care to theater. Eric would miss his family but decided that this sounded like fun. He would be away for four whole weeks, longer than he had ever been gone before. Archie, now five, was crestfallen. He counted on Eric as his daily playmate; now who would chase him around the house, or build stuff to knock down, or peek out of hiding places and yell "Boo"? My husband and I, on the other hand, tried to imagine the ensuing quiet.

As it turned out, they all missed Eric—even the two brothers who had hardly ever seemed to want to bother with him. Of course, now both were older and shared a bond of serious interest in music, but there was no one to come into the room and bop anyone on the arm or start some excitement. It was relatively quiet for four weeks, with the fun arriving in the form of Eric's letters—one with a few spent cartridges from the camp's riflery range, another with some gravel he had found interesting—both addressed to his youngest brother, who thought them true treasures. It was entirely too peaceful without Eric.

Back home, Eric dumped his duffel bag of dirty laundry in the living room and began to open some other rumpled packages. First came a bright yellow stuffed animal—or creature of uncertain species—a wonderful, whimsical companion for a boy's room. He had made it himself, along with a color-splashed pair of Bermuda shorts that *did* actually fit him. (In an improbable flash of fantasy, I began to see my mending pile diminish, with the aid of Eric's new skill.) Then, Eric began to peel back layers of newspaper, encasing what looked like a large box of some sort. What emerged from its wrappings was a good-sized wooden bookshelf, stained a dark mahogany color, and fitted with two sliding doors with finger-holes carefully bored into them.

"It's for you, Mom." Eric proudly presented his masterpiece. "I worked on it the whole time."

My eyes began to well up, but I managed to remark, "How beautiful! I'll have to find just the right place to put it." Only then did I notice something unusual about the shelf—each of the corners was carefully sanded down flat.

Eric followed my eyes and said, "Oh, you can put it anywhere, Mom. I took off all the corners so Archie wouldn't hurt himself on it if he fell."

I smiled with a sudden sense of gratitude, realizing what soul mates these two brothers were—how well they knew and loved each other and understood each other's needs. My sentimental moment was to be short-lived, however, for the minute he had shown off his new treasures, Eric tore out of the room running after his younger brother. "Chasing time" was back, and it was music to my ears.

Batman Kisses

Michael T. Powers

M Y FOUR-YEAR-OLD SON, Caleb, thinks he's Batman. Not a day goes by that he doesn't put his Batman suit on and try to make the world a safer place for us to live in. It all started last Halloween when we took him shopping to pick out a costume, and he insisted that he must be Batman. We found a costume that fit him for $19.95, but it was not the Batman suit of the recent blockbuster movies with its reinforced armor and sleek, aerodynamic look. No, this was the kind Adam West wore in the TV series some thirty years ago, the one where his not-so-athletic belly stuck out and only a pair of tights covered his legs.

Caleb has worn the costume so much that it is torn, stained, and won't tie around his neck anymore, but the more tattered it becomes, the more he has grown to love it. I'm sure that one of our favorite memories years from now will be Caleb throwing his arms and one leg back, pausing dramatically, and then "whooshing" into the next room, cape billowing behind him as he fights crime in our Wisconsin home.

Caleb constantly bugs me to play Batman, and when I am able, I play along with him. I'd like to claim that I only do it because I love my son and want to spend time with him, which is the case most of the time. However, to be totally honest, I was also a four-year-old who loved to play Batman back in the early 1970s, and I must admit, I have as much fun playing Batman now as my boy does.

There's one thing I love to do when we play Batman—regardless of which villain I am. Sometimes I'm a traditional bad-guy like the Joker or the Penguin; however, sometimes I am the tickle-monster, and sometimes Caleb just calls me the daddy-monster. But whichever role I assume, there is one "trick" that must be played on him. In the middle of the fight, I throw him down on the waterbed, get on top of him, and then plant a thousand kisses on his face.

The first time I did this, Caleb looked at me in pure shock. I guess it was the last thing he expected the Joker to do to him. He can deal with play punches and kicks—he blocks them or tries to roll out of the way. Pillows sent flying his way can be avoided by ducking . . . but kisses? Especially kisses from his archenemy? How does Batman deal with that?

There is no kiss repellent on his utility belt. So after the look of disbelief passed, another look took over—a look that can only be described as total and outright betrayal. "Daddy, how could you?" I imagine him thinking. "How could you defile something as sacred as playing Batman . . . by kissing me?"

The last time I planted daddy kisses on his chubby cheeks, he just froze, peering up at me with that stunned look on his face, then rolled his eyes and screamed, "Daaaaddy! You don't give kisses while you are playing Batman!"

Oh, how I laughed! He has since become smarter in his dealings with my villainous kisses during our Batman sessions. Now, whenever I start to kiss him, he points to the Batman logo on his chest and shoots a bat-ray right at me.

"I'm turning you back into the Joker, Daddy."

He figures that these unforgivable lapses into daddy-hood can be reversed with his special Batman powers. I usually play along with him and immediately switch back to the traditional role of the villain—unless, that is, I am especially in the kissy mood.

Sadly, the Batman costume has seen its last days. We will be retiring it very soon and most likely replacing it with a new one. In fact, we'll probably look for the suit that's based on the more recent Batman movies and hopefully, it will be a little higher quality and last a little longer than the previous costume. When we do, however, I'll be taking the old, ripped, worn-out suit and will be setting it aside in a special place— the place reserved for magical childhood memories . . . and for things to show his first girlfriend.

Although I realize that these precious times with my son are as fleeting as water flowing through cupped hands, I know that in the future I'll take the suit out from time to time to try to recapture the early years of my son's life. When I am done reminiscing, I'll place the suit back in its hiding place, but not before wiping the tears from my eyes.

I am determined, though, that my tears will be those of happy remembrance, and not of the regret of wishing I had spent more time with my children.

Here's one last kiss, Batman . . .

PART TWO

Defining Moments

"There is always one moment in childhood when the door opens and lets the
future in."

—Graham Greene

The Red Bike

Barbara Workinger

WHEN MY SON, Robert, or Robbie as we called him then, was seven, we finally saw some hope for his future. Until then, he had proven himself to be cute, lovable, and an expert at getting one of his three older sisters to do his chores.

I had visions of his future filled with women used for such nefarious purposes as tutoring him through high school then cast aside. His career choices would lie between actor, gigolo, and perhaps, if the tutoring had been expert, college professor. He would then move to using graduate students to do his research. If he was especially adept at manipulating students, he would be widely published and famous. If his reputation for treating his graduate assistants badly became known, he would have to settle for mildly notorious. Perhaps he might then aspire to department chair. He could occupy himself with watching the ivy grow outside his office window. It was not exactly the future we had hoped for our only son.

The turning point came without warning. One sultry summer day, Robbie turned from his favorite spot, a beanbag chair in front of the television. The girls were out somewhere usefully occupying their summer vacation, and I was staring into the refrigerator hoping to be inspired into a dinner worthy of Julia Child but knowing it would actually be Chef Boyardee and a salad that night.

"Mom! I'm going to get a bike," Robbie shouted, jumping to his feet. I closed the avocado green door of my refrigerator and turned to look at my son, who was showing an unusual amount of animation. The stripes on his T-shirt were undulating in rhythm to his bouncing body.

"Honey," I said, in my calmest June Cleaver voice. "You have a bike." We had had the same discussion for the last six months, since he had inherited his older sister's bike. I knew the scenario well.

"Mom, it's a girl's bike."

"No, it is not. It has a bar across it. Amy rode a boy's bike, and she didn't complain."

He would then break into a monologue about how her very ownership of said bicycle made it a girl's bike and launch into the bike having cooties or maybe it was his sister who had the cooties. Anyhow, cooties were involved in the argument somewhere. The final straw was that everybody knew it was his sister's old bike, and no kid anywhere in the world except him had to ride an old, used girl's bike. With cooties. We were at an impasse with the matter of Amy's bike. Robbie went on a bike strike. He would not ride it.

"No, Mom, you don't understand. I am going to *win* a bike," my son said, gesturing at the television screen. "From Captain Zero's show."

The television show he was referring to originated from a town ninety miles away but was bright and clear by our rabbit ears. "See. See," he said pointing to the set. A 1970's version of a children's television host, girdled into a silver jumpsuit, was speaking in the voice reserved for children and animals. "Yes siree, boys and girls, you will get a brand-new, fire-engine-red bike in your choice of models. The winner of our fire prevention poster contest will be one lucky little astronaut. Just send that poster to our station by this Friday." It was Monday now. Five days to produce the poster and get it to Sacramento. "Just have Mom or Dad copy down the instructions on our screen at the end of the program and lots of luck to you, boys and girls."

I looked at the faraway look on Robbie's face. He was already riding that shiny, red, cootie-free, boy's bike up and down our suburban street. Dutifully, I copied the rules, which stayed on the screen at least three minutes. Parents or guardian had to swear and attest to the poster being the child's idea and it must be the entrant's original "concept and work."

I tried to explain this to Robbie and, more important, tell him there would be a lot of kids entering posters. A lot of much older kids. The contest was for kids from six to fourteen. *Not fair,* silently protested the mother in me. I wasn't even sure he would get it there in time.

In my mind's eye, I was envisioning the contest's outcome. We would have a shattered child. He might be so traumatized he would ride the cootie bike or, more realistically, my husband and I would break down and buy him a new bike.

Robbie was only half listening to my warnings. He would not be dissuaded or discouraged, but instead dashed into his room to return shortly with a drawing pad and a box of colored pencils, which he spread out on the little-used dining room table.

An hour later he was still there. He had now graduated to poster-size paper from his easel. He was breaking his record for concentrating on one subject that did not involve television or sister-torment.

"How are you doing?" I asked.

"Good," he reported cheerfully, "but here is a list of stuff I'm gonna need," he said, handing me a piece of paper. His spelling, at seven, was hard to decipher. "Tell me about the things," I asked, remembering the lesson learned with the girls of not to stifle creativity by correcting spelling.

"String, wire, fuzzy cloth, red 'cefalane,' lots of tape. I need some of those big poster boards you had for the garage sale."

I asked a few questions and went to gather the supplies. I figured this was not against contest rules. I was pretty amazed at his list and how much quick thought he'd put into the project.

Robbie worked industriously all afternoon, even skipping the highlight of every seven-year-old's afternoon, snack time. When I tried to look at the project, he covered it with another piece of paper. Artistic temperament, I assumed.

When the girls arrived home, he was in the dining room with the door closed. During the afternoon, he had come out three times, twice to ask my help in wire cutting and cutting material. The final time concerned a twig-gathering foray into the yard. I watched him patiently measuring twigs against each other and choosing carefully. When the girls arrived home from scout day camp, I explained their brother was making a poster and what the prize was for first place. Their reactions ranged from groans to piteous looks of empathy.

Naturally, all three girls were curious to see what the outcome would be. No one was more curious than I. Visions of the thing falling apart when he lifted it up filled my head. My husband was out of town on business, so I steeled myself to be appropriately supportive if my son's project was a miserable failure. It would be good practice for the day when the winners were announced, I thought gloomily. I stuffed my pockets with tissues, ready for the onslaught of disappointed tears.

A few minutes before dinner, the sliding pocket door to the dining room shuddered open, heightening the drama of the moment. From a table piled high with the debris of the project, my son carefully held up his creation. For a briefest second, no one spoke.

In his hands he held what even I, prejudiced as I was, realized was an original, charming, and creative poster. Still, he had a long way to go in competition to win that bike.

In the poster, a fuzzy bear in a felt hat was holding a bucket composed of foil-covered cardboard with a wire handle. To the right of the bear was a twig campfire overlaid with the red cellophane Robbie had requested. The proportions were amazingly accurate for a seven-year-old.

"That is really good, Robbie. Really," one of the girls said, and her sentiments were echoed by the rest of us.

"It isn't exactly right," Robbie announced when the din had died down.

Oh, no, I thought, maybe the glue won't hold or it will all fall apart.

"It does stuff," he said. "But, Mom, you have to twist the wire for me. See, look at the back."

I walked gingerly around the poster and saw the back side of it. He had a piece of wire attached behind the silver bucket handle and it dangled free in the back.

"See, I need to have a loop so the bucket will move a little and it has to reach to the top so Captain Zero can get his hand in there to move it. It has to be a big loop 'cause he wears those big gloves."

My son might not understand the judging process, but he had an instinctive idea of engineering principles, or was it physics principles? Obviously, it was not a gene he had inherited from me. I added a few twists to his poster, not worrying one bit if I was breaking any rules. *Better a broken rule than a brokenhearted little boy,* I thought.

He pulled on the wire and the bucket moved. Nothing fell apart or off. My girls cheered and clapped. After the noise died down, I reminded him it still might not get there in time.

"Oh, Mom," my teenage daughter said in what I called her "poor pitiful mom voice." "We can drive to Sacramento tomorrow and deliver it. That's easy." We did, and it was. My son's hazel eyes sparkled as he handed the poster to the woman at the information desk. We signed the required forms, and the precious poster was whisked out of sight.

All that week, Rob watched the television while Captain

Zero continued to announce the contest and mention how many, many entries were coming in. As the totals rose, my hopes for Robbie's project plummeted. How could a seven-year-old compete with the proficient work of a child twice his age?

Robbie's faith in his special poster never wavered, and only once during the week did he say anything to indicate he knew there was a slight chance of not winning.

"If I didn't win this year, Mom, I'll win next year. I got a plan. Just in case."

I felt much better about his ability to deal with disappointment. At least he had a dash of realism in his optimism.

The weekend went by and Monday afternoon arrived. My husband managed to get home early. Day camp was over for the younger girls, and even my teenager abandoned her friends and stayed around for the announcement. Our family room took on the air of a hospital waiting room. My husband paced; I thumbed through a magazine without reading a word of it; the girls chattered; and Robbie sat in his beanbag chair, uncharacteristically still.

We had to endure Captain Zero's patter for twenty minutes before he got to the big moment. I literally held my breath, preparing myself for the moans and possible tears and one very disappointed little boy. Captain Zero began by announcing the honorable mentions who would receive certificates from the fire department. Reeling off the names and ages took several minutes. So many older ones, I thought, my heart sinking. Robbie's name wasn't on the list.

"As you remember," Captain Zero intoned, "there are no third or second places, but everyone who entered will receive a Captain Zero patch. Now boys and girls, all of your entries were just great! All will be displayed in local firehouses."

My husband was muttering under his breath by now. "Get on with it," I heard him say to the television. Would that Captain Zero could hear him. I, too, wanted this to be over.

"It was very hard for the judges to decide, but we have found one poster that was so creative, it was the unanimous choice for top prize. The winner is . . ." Then Captain Zero said Robbie's name, age, and hometown. "Wonderful job, Robert! I'm looking forward to shaking your hand when you pick up your brand-new red boy's bike, donated by Bill and Barry's Hardware." Captain Zero's voice boomed from the screen.

Our family room erupted with shouts and squeals. Robbie sat like the calm center of the storm, as self-possessed as an adult, although I could swear there was a glint of triumph in his eyes.

That episode marked a turning point in my son's life and how the rest of the family regarded him. I stopped worrying about his future. To this day, he still has the creative spark and determination to make things work for him. And what of the red bike? It hangs in my son's suburban garage. His little girl can't wait until she is old enough to ride it. She doesn't seem to mind it's a 1970's boy's model, and she has never heard of cooties.

Stretch Marks

Sara Camilli

GOING INTO MOTHERHOOD, I always envisioned myself as a teacher and mentor. But looking back now that our three sons are grown, I realize how much I learned from them. They taught me boldness and daring. They took risks I never would have dreamed of and took me to places I never would have ventured. Though they always tried to follow their parents' lead, they recognized that sometimes parents needed to be led. They stretched us, and we grew into better, more interesting people as a result.

Our first son, Michael, started a neighborhood newspaper, *The Gray Street Gazette,* when he was ten years old. When he first broached the idea, I thought of the difficulties involved in such a pursuit. How will you print it? It will take so much time and work. He overlooked my discouraging statements and welcomed the interesting challenge. He and his younger brother Keith happily went off to interview neighbors armed with a Polaroid camera. He composed articles on the typewriter and pasted them on a page to be photocopied by a friend who donated that service. Neighbors happily bought the finished product that told of new people on the block, new babies, birthdays, job advancements, and so on for the princely sum of 25 cents each. Someone soon suggested that the boys get advertisers, and when they sold an ad to a local restaurant that featured a $1.00 off coupon, the boys were ecstatic to have a woman from a nearby street bicycle over to buy four copies so she could get the coupons. Now they were real entrepreneurs! Soon the public library heard of the venture and asked if it could be included on the subscription list. One of the librarians later reported that many children loved to come in and see a paper written by other children. The paper continued for 2½ years, and the boys gained many valuable lessons from the experience. Their parents learned even more.

Keith, our second son, enjoyed digging up old bottles with one of his friends. When we moved to an area where there weren't as many places to dig, he started attending auctions to find bottles to add to his growing collection. But it seemed that they often came in box lots that contained many things besides the desired bottles. When I encouraged Keith to get rid of some of the extras, he became curious about some of the items he had acquired. With some research in the library, he learned about mercury glass, depression glass, and peach-blow glass. What Mother considered trash now became cherished treasure, and the whole family learned about the artifacts. Alas, the family garage was bursting at the seams with his extra collection. So as we talked about it, he decided to start his own antique business. He was 15 years old and had homework, track, swimming, and so on. You guessed it, I wasn't at all encouraging about this new venture, but he joined an antique co-op anyway and worked there through high school, college, and his first job. When he went away to graduate school, his newly converted mother took it over for him until his return. I now not only know a fair amount about antiques, I enjoy the hunt for hidden treasures myself. And this has been a special interest for Keith and his mom to share— time together we probably would not have otherwise had.

The baby of the bunch, Stephen, has stretched us, too— but more geographically than the others. He went to Argentina as a Rotary Ambassadorial student. While there, he was touched by the poverty and hunger he found when he volunteered in one of the poorer sections of Buenos Aires. Across the miles, he told us of his desire to start a food bank, common in the United States, but nonexistent there. Our reaction, of course, was, "Stephen, what can one person do?" And he went on to show us! We now know that one person really *can* make a difference. The food bank is up and running, and last month it distributed $1/4$ million pounds of food. I suggested Stephen use the spouses of ex-pat workers as volunteers in the facility. He wisely negated my suggestion, saying, "It is in Argentina. It must be run by Argentines to be successful." Now he hopes to start a foundation or nonprofit organization to set up food banks in other countries in need, such as Uruguay and Chile.

When parents start on the journey of raising sons, they

never imagine what lies on the path ahead. They imagine themselves being the leaders. For a time, we do lead by example, but our bright, strong sons soon surpass us on the journey and we become the followers. Isn't that the dream of every teacher—that their student will become better than they?

After all these years of training, the boys have finally gotten their lessons across. I no longer question that it can be done. I just wonder how long it will take.

Eyes to See

Rebecca R. Howell

"I HAVE SOMETHING THAT is red and round, that rhymes with 'doll,'" I said to my second-grade son, David. "It is a . . ."

The silence dragged on as he pondered the question. David's rhythm was different from mine. One minute . . . two minutes . . . how long could I possibly sit waiting? My patience wearing thin, I breathed a silent sigh of relief when finally, "Ball?" came tentatively from him.

"Right. Good. Now, pick up your pencil and write it on the line here. B-A-L-L. Good. Now, let's do the next question." A homework assignment that was supposed to take ten minutes would take more than an hour. I knew all children were different, but it seemed to me that some were more different than others. The psychologists called it a "central processing problem." David said it felt like his brain was just lazy. Whatever it was, it was driving me crazy.

Then one day I received a gift. The gift was a lesson in who my son really was. And this gift would sustain me as David's mother for many years to come. As we drove to the orthodontist in the city that Tuesday afternoon, he began to quiz me on orchestra trivia—the difference between a valve trombone and a slide trombone, and could I name three different woodwinds and four different stringed instruments in order of size? Detail after detail, and he knew all the answers cold.

Stopping at a gift shop that sold African artifacts, he quizzed the shopkeeper on Egyptian mythology: Who was Osiris, what was Ra the god of, and could he identify them from their pictures?

Pointing to some abstract sculptures of animals and people in the store, David remarked, "Those sculptures remind me of Picasso, Mommy." And they did. But David had been to see the Picasso exhibit two years before—when he was only five!

So there it was. David's eye—the way he saw things, his vision, his interpretation of the world around him; his ear—the way he heard music, his ability to remember details about things he was interested in. Clearly, he had intelligence beyond his years. But I had gotten caught up in the painstaking process of helping David learn to *read* and *write* and had somehow lost track of the fact that in other areas, he was a very bright, curious, and involved child who learned many things well. In fact, he saw connections in the world better than most adults. I realized that day it was *my* eyes that needed opening, not his.

And, as I promised him over and over in those early years, David *did* eventually learn to read, and to read well. It just took a little more time and a lot more work from him and from me and from his teachers. After the trip to the city that day, I was able to remember and focus on the fact that David was much more than his weaknesses.

Today, he is in high school with dreams of being an actor. He might make it. Whatever he does, though, it will be done with the special spark of different-ness that has always been part of who David is.

Hearing Evan's Voice

Ann Reuthling

ONCE AGAIN, I HAD left my holiday shopping until the last minute. It was a cold, crisp December day, and I was walking across the parking lot to my car, feet aching and arms loaded with packages. The strip mall consisted of several neighborhood stores—a card shop, an ice-cream parlor, a small movie theater, a pet store, and several fast-food restaurants. As I reached my car, I heard a strangely familiar voice over a loudspeaker. It was calling out, "Number 72, your order is ready."

I had momentarily forgotten that my son, Evan, was working at his new job that afternoon, but when I heard the voice, something stirred inside me. You see, the voice was Evan's. He was apparently working the order pick-up counter at Rubio's Fish Tacos (his new employer), and it was his voice booming over the microphone. It was so odd to hear it, and the mother in me did a double-take. Here was my son—at his first real job—hopefully giving good service to all the patrons and smiling at them with that beautiful smile of his.

How can that be my little boy? I wondered. How can he be six feet tall already? It was just a couple years ago that his favorite thing to do was to stand in our driveway in his diapers and wave to all the garbage men as they came down our street every Thursday. It was all I could do, now, to keep from slipping quietly into his restaurant under cover and watch Evan in action. But mustering all the self-control a mother needs in a situation like this, I opted to sit in my car for a few minutes and just listen to Evan's voice . . . and my heart.

Immersed in a sense of protectiveness and pride, the Mother Bear in me wanted everyone to know that the boy behind the loudspeaker was my child. And that he wasn't just another kid behind a counter—he was a good person who wouldn't hurt a fly. I sat there hoping that, in the process of getting people their orders, Evan would have an occasion to share his gentle, quick wit and his genuine, down-to-earth nature with customers, and that their interaction would leave the people in a little better place than they were before they'd met Evan. I wanted mostly, though, something quite basic: I wanted him to be kind and respectful to his customers and for them to be kind and respectful in return. That thought made my heart heavy as I pondered what it was about this world that makes such a hope for a child—for anyone—even necessary in the first place.

Sitting in the car and feeling so moved and protective as

Evan's voice resounded through the parking lot, I had an interesting thought: Each and every person is someone's child. And whether that child is now old or young, rich or poor, friendly or angry—whether he's a police officer, a politician, a factory worker, or a rock star—someone once cradled him tenderly as a baby, taught him to look both ways before crossing the street, and comforted him when he was scared of the dark. And I hoped, as only a parent can hope, that life would be good to him.

Since the day I heard Evan's voice in that new way, I look at everyone a little differently. And I try to remember the child in every man.

The Disguise

Sharon Brody

IT ISN'T THAT I want my children to be normal, exactly.

I'm proud of their eccentricities, but every year, along about late October, I begin to wonder if it wouldn't be sweet to see how the other half live. You know which half: the parents who obediently plod to Wal-Mart and buy Halloween costumes off the rack for their media-saturated, trend-obsessed children. Wouldn't that be unbelievably easy?

Oh, of course, in theory I prefer my sons' quirky individuality in the face of mass-produced rubbish. But it *is* more work. On Halloweens past, my third-grader and kindergartner have commanded me to transform them into an oscillating fan, Thomas Jefferson, a boy wearing a hat with grapes on it, and a decommissioned model of a Boston green line trolley. I thought I was prepared for anything when my eight-year-old announced his Halloween plans. Not a costume like Pikachu, the Pokémon character achieving total world domination for my trick-or-treater. No, my son told me that he needs to become . . . a . . . car. For Halloween, he says, he must be a light green Saturn station wagon, model year 1993–1995.

I am trying not to freak. For one thing, I cannot possibly create this getup, seeing as I have all the arts and crafts ability of a liverwort. But what truly terrifies me is my son! What is his problem? Why does he care about Saturns? Good grief, he has only just learned to ride a two-wheeler. Has the kid managed to escape the omnipotent blitz of a gazillion-dollar juvenile marketing industry . . . only to fall victim to stupid commercials for grown-ups? Has he bypassed childhood fads to move directly into big-ticket adult items? What is he gonna want for his ninth birthday? His-and-her Rolexes? An eBay account? A Carnival Cruise Line vacation? My God, have the marketers no shame? Are they now zeroing in on a population that can barely tie its own shoes? My son is eight years old! He has no disposable income. *Why are you trying to sell him a sensible American-made family wagon?*

Hyperventilating, I grabbed my little Saturn-head by his skinny shoulders and demanded to know just what ersatz folksy automotive brainwashing he's succumbed to . . . or words to that effect. His answer? And this is a direct quote: "I just noticed one day that the old Saturn station wagon has recessed headlights. And I really like that."

Oh.

Recessed headlights.

He's just being his usual weird self. No Madison Avenue youth loyalty conspiracy in sight. Just recessed headlights. It's just his thing.

Overreact much? Me? Nope, no way, never, not this mom. Not at all.

A New Form of Praise

Lissa Lee

IF YOU EVER HAVE the good fortune of traveling south of the Mason-Dixon line, count yourself blessed. But if you are given the divine privilege to be invited to attend an African-American church, don't even hesitate—accept immediately!

Through the casual acquaintance with my oldest son's kindergarten teacher, I got the invitation of a lifetime. She invited us to attend a "singing" at her Methodist Church. I was flattered and accepted immediately.

For the most part, I had spent a great deal of my life in a Southern Baptist church. We dressed rather formally on Sunday mornings, but I had been warned earlier in the week that black people usually dressed up for church. Bearing that in mind, my three children and I put on our "Sunday best," believing this was adequate, and off we went.

I had no trouble locating the church. Finding a place to park was another story. The church lot was full. And I suddenly realized we were the only white people for miles around. Two elegantly dressed young men directed me through a maze of parked cars to a spot underneath a large leafy oak. They opened my car door and offered their arm to my daughter and me. Telling my three young sons to stay close, they escorted us in through the doors, down the center aisle, and seated us on the front row of their church auditorium.

I wasn't prepared for what came next. The music stopped and the entire congregation seated in my general vicinity smiled, extended a hand, and introduced themselves. The pastor asked my name and announced to the whole congregation how pleased he was for me to join them this afternoon. *So much for quietly blending in*, I thought. These people not only welcomed me and my children, they set us in the place of honor. It was then that I noticed how exquisitely everyone was dressed and how "frumpy" we looked.

Everyone was in the height of fashion. The men were adorned in immaculately tailored suits with complementary neckties and pocket hankies. Their shoes were polished so brightly they twinkled. The women were simply gorgeous. Everyone had on a coordinated suit or ensemble that was topped with an elegant hat, gloves, and matching shoes and handbag. I had never seen so many brilliantly clothed individuals in one place.

Finally the singing started, and the music was wonderful. I was beginning to relax and enjoy the afternoon. One of the groups to perform was the teacher's trio. When these women opened their mouths, they filled the room with the most perfectly blended a cappella harmonies I had ever heard. It was angelic.

I felt my tense body go limp. My fear of the new experience evaporated. I gathered my sleepy daughter into my arms and settled her on my lap. My oldest son leaned against my shoulder, and my middle son perched on his knees and stared out across the faces of the people in the rows behind us. Everything was perfect.

The next song was a favorite of the congregation. The ladies finished the first verse, and then it happened. As was the custom, the people produced elegant white lacey handkerchiefs, which they extended and began waving gently in the air as a signal to the singers to continue the song.

Fascinated by the strange new custom, I was paying no attention to my four-year-old son, David. Wanting to be a part of the festivities, he looked in my purse and found the first white thing he could. He took out a Kotex pad and began waving it in the air just like the women waving their handkerchiefs. Apparently, David liked this new church and thought this hanky thing was great fun.

Okay, so I'm the only white woman in the whole building. My son is sitting on the front row in plain view of the whole congregation, wildly waving a Kotex in the air, and I'm staring straight ahead, praying no one will notice. Right. Muffled laughter began breaking out like microwave popcorn. Despite their best efforts to continue the song, even the trio began to giggle. Paralysis took over and I had no idea what to do next.

Recognizing my predicament, a sweet woman in the row behind reached up and gently confiscated the pad from

David's hand and passed it to me. I smiled a nervous smile, thanked her, and shoved it quickly into my purse.

My son, not knowing the depth of my humiliation, began a little boy's pleading to have the pad back so he could wave it like the ladies were doing. And he wouldn't stop, no matter how much I gave him the "evil eye." *Come on brain— think of something quick*, I heard myself whisper.

My solution? Make a beeline to my car, dragging three confused boys behind me, all asking—out loud!—why we had to leave.

The next day, my son's teacher and I had a long laugh. She said it was the funniest thing that had ever happened in that church, and they'd be talking about it for years. I knew I would be, too, just not with the same perspective.

So if you ever get to visit an African-American church in the rural South—go. But remember two very important things: Dress to kill, and lock up all your feminine hygiene products from the unsuspecting hands of four-year-old boys!

The Lesson of the Lightning Bugs

Michael T. Powers

O N THE FOURTH OF July, my wife, Kristi, and I took our little boy a couple blocks from our house to a huge hill where we could enjoy the fireworks, from our town and neighboring towns as well. It was a hot night, but there was a wonderful breeze, and we could see a long way in all directions.

I wanted to see our three-year-old Caleb's reaction to the fireworks. He sat with us all of two minutes before he started tumbling down the hill and giggling.

"Caleb, come here." He would reluctantly come back by us and sit for a spell. "See the pretty colors over there?"

"Oooohhh!" he replied, all the while looking in a different direction from where the fireworks were actually going off. "Hee hee!" He giggled as he tumbled down the steep hill again.

"Caleb, come here and watch with Daddy."

"Okay, Daddy."

Back up the hill he would climb, where I tried getting him to concentrate on the fireworks again. He watched for another twenty seconds before he started walking away from us. Suddenly, he let out a squeal of delight. *Finally!* I thought, *He's finally enjoying the fireworks.* And then Caleb yelled out, "Look at all the lightning bugs!"

I sighed and looked down the hill; indeed, there were literally hundreds of fireflies that were stealing Daddy's thunder. But fireflies were nothing compared to the spectacular fireworks show, and after all, this was the Fourth of July—the only day of the year we'd have fireworks! I tried in vain one last time to get him to watch with me. "Caleb, tell me what colors you see up in the sky."

"That's a green one, Daddy! And a red one!" This lasted another minute or so before he reached in the stroller to tickle Connor, his eleven-month-old brother. Then he was off tumbling down the hill again, saying, "Whoa, whoa, whoa," with each spin of his body. I started to call out to him again when Kristi leaned over to me and whispered, "Michael, just let him be a kid. There will be other years."

I knew she was right. I was so irritated that he wouldn't sit by us and take in the fireworks that I had forgotten to enjoy the moment. I guess I had some preconceived notion that he would sit on my lap and squeal with delight every time the fireworks exploded. Then he'd ask me if they were magic, and I, his proud and smart Daddy, would stick out my chest and explain away. Luckily, my understanding wife was there and was able to gently nudge me back to reality. There was nothing wrong with my expectations, but my impatience was getting in the way of enjoying the time with my wife and sons. Instead, I should've picked up on the cues and tumbled down the hill with my boy. Fireworks have been around for hundreds of years, but my boy was only going to be three years old for another week.

I bet when a person tumbles down the hill, the lightning bugs actually look like fireworks going off anyway. Maybe we'll start a new tradition for the Fourth of July.

Actually, from what my three-year-old tells me, the show goes on every night!

PART THREE

Pink and Blue

"My son and daughter tell me where they are in very different ways. I know where my son is because I hear him. I know where my daughter is because she tells me."

—Anonymous

The Balancing Act

Cheryl Erwin

PHILIP LOVED BASEBALL. When he was two, he and his dad would play in the backyard with a plastic bat and a whiffle ball. Every time the bat contacted the ball, no matter how gently, it was a "home run" and Philip delighted in touring the backyard, his small legs pumping like chubby pistons. At three, he knew the entire starting lineup of the San Francisco Giants and could point out each player at spring training; by four, he had learned to read by matching the names and faces he knew with the words on his baseball cards.

So it was no surprise that Philip wanted to play baseball when he got older. Beginning with T-ball at five years old, Philip progressed through the stages of Little League. Nevada's chilly spring weather always found me huddled under a blanket with the other moms and dads, watching yet another practice or cheering the boys on in another game as spring turned to summer.

When Philip was six years old, his dad and I divorced. It was a painful time for all of us, but somehow the rhythm of the seasons smoothed out the rough edges of our lives. Spring always came again, and with it another baseball season.

Being the single mother of the most cheerful and loving little boy isn't always easy, though. There are so many subtle messages in our culture telling boys that being "too close" to their moms isn't quite healthy, phrases like "tied to the apron strings" or "mama's boy." Philip and I had a close and loving relationship, and although he seemed to be a happy, independent, and self-reliant young man, I sometimes wondered if I had the balance right. Too close? Too distant? It didn't help that my former mother-in-law tsk-tsk'd frequently when Philip gave me a hug. "You're too close," she said. "You're making him dependent on you."

It isn't always easy to know what's right, as any parent can attest. One summer afternoon at the baseball park suddenly revealed just how difficult knowing what to do can be. Philip was about ten; by now, he was the starting catcher for his team, the Mariners. He had never been the most physically gifted player in the league, but he compensated with sheer love of the game and hard work, practicing his throws from home plate to second base with patience and dedication.

The game was tied on this particular afternoon, and the opposing team was at bat with the bases loaded. Philip was crouched behind the plate, as usual, his mask pulled down over his face. The batter pegged a bouncing ball to the shortstop, who turned and threw to Philip as the runner on third dashed for home plate. Sliding headfirst isn't allowed in Little League, but in the heat of the moment and the desire to score the winning run, the runner, still wearing his batting helmet, forgot. He threw himself forward, while Philip did what all catchers are supposed to do: He moved forward to receive the throw and block the plate. There was a sickening crunch and a cloud of dust; when it cleared, the runner was leaving the field—called out by the umpire—and my son was lying still in the dirt, the ball clutched in his glove and a small trickle of blood running down his cheek.

I was on my feet immediately. But before I could turn to leave my seat, the man sitting next to me placed his hand on my arm and gently but quite firmly pulled me down. "He doesn't want you out there," he said. "Let the coaches handle it."

To my everlasting shame, I sank slowly into my seat. I watched, numb, while the coaches helped Philip up and walked him to the dugout, while the assembled players and parents gave him the obligatory round of applause. Then I saw my son looking at the fence and realized who it was he was searching for. Again I was on my feet, and this time I didn't hesitate.

What is it that we're teaching our young men? That it is weakness to need comfort or encouragement? That "real men" don't want their mothers' affection or support? It would not have been helpful for me to rush onto the field or to embarrass my son, but it didn't help much for me to stay nailed to my seat, either. The truth is that being close to a mother doesn't make a boy weak any more than being close to a father makes him strong. Our sons need all the best their mothers and fathers have to give: our encouragement and affection, our faith and our support, our wisdom and our patience. Boys need closeness and contact just as much as they need faith and space to become themselves. Like so many things in parenting, the answer isn't one or the other—it's a balance of both.

By the time I reached the fence behind the dugout, Philip was sitting on the bench with ice on his lip. "Hey, Bud," I said with a smile, "how are you feeling?"

His chin trembled a bit, but his voice and his gaze were steady. "I'm okay—I just cut my lip." Then he added softly, "Thanks, Mom."

Philip is now almost eighteen years old, getting ready to graduate from high school and move on to college, testing the wings he's so anxious to try. He is a confident young man who has done well in school, earned the rank of Eagle Scout, worked hard enough to buy his own truck, and has a close group of friends. He gave up baseball for golf a couple years ago, so those days of sitting in the bleachers are gone. My job now is to watch and cheer as he begins his own journey through life. I am happy to report, however, that despite his growing independence and obvious ability to take care of himself, he never leaves the house without giving his mom a hug.

Super Bowl Challenged

Karin Kasdin

IT IS RUMORED that babies choose their mothers from heaven before they are born. If this is indeed the case, I can only surmise that my two oldest sons' first-choice mother—the mother who skis and surfs and understands the rules of football—was in the loo during the lineup. Twice! Or perhaps I was on the mother clearance rack. Or perhaps the surfer-skier-football-understander mother was in fact standing right in front of me but ducked twice . . . just when my babies pointed at her, leading God to erroneously believe that it was sedentary little me whom they wanted to call Mommy. Somewhere there are a couple curly-haired girls who are as miserable backpacking in the mountains with their mommy as my sons, Dan and Andrew, have been sitting in theaters next to me. Apparently, the customer service department where babies come from has been in dire need of an overhaul for a long time. My oldest sons are now twenty and sixteen.

I placed orders for girls *three times* because of preconceived notions I had about boys, both little and big. They are noisy. They think passing gas is funny. And they enjoy watching, participating in, and attending sporting events where they can be noisy *and* pass gas *and* get hysterical all at once. Okay, so this is a stereotype, and I am an educated, liberal woman who should know better than to cling to outdated notions of masculinity and femininity. Frankly though, my sons never did one thing to help me blast any myths.

Each of the first two came out of the womb kicking and, twenty years later, have yet to cease and desist. Mostly they kick balls. Often they kick each other. They turn everything into competition. Tic-tac-toe, when played in our home, is a blood sport. The boys forced me into signing them up for soccer, tennis, basketball, and baseball. The writing of those checks is the closest I have ever gotten to participation in team activities. My husband, Harold, though born a genuine male, is no better than I am when it comes to organized sports but is a whole lot better than me at the disorganized ones. He loves the beach, and at the age of fifty-two can still bodysurf with the teenagers. He's not a "gray on a tray," which is what the young and hip affectionately call adults who snowboard, but I'd definitely call him a "geez on skis." Still, if you ask him what a third down is, he'll invariably think mortgage before football.

Neither of us knew how to keep score in a tennis match until Dan became an ace. Neither of us had ever attended a professional baseball game until Andrew became a pariah in the third grade because he'd never seen the Phillies live. Harold's favorite part about the game we attended was standing in line for the hot dogs. And that was the year the Phillies made it to the World Series. We heard the games were really exciting!

There was a time I believed I could pilot my children's proclivities as well as their behaviors merely by exposing them to my own. Today, after stretching and molding and manipulating and imploring, after trying to squeeze each of them into a mold I had concocted in my head of the perfect boy (more accurately, the perfect "unboy"), I understand the futility of it all. You can teach your child to say please and thank you when appropriate, but you can't teach him to prefer *Masterpiece Theater* to *Baywatch*.

I believe Dan and Andrew love us very much, but I also believe that we disappointed them in some fundamental ways. While other boys took batting practice in their backyards with their dads, ours were dragged to museums and art shows and historical sites. My hope was to ignite in them a love of culture that would continue to enrich their lives well after their knees gave out. *Ha!* They'll embrace high culture only when it rides into their lives on a wave.

Then came Zack. Ten years after the birth of my first son, the baby girls up in heaven still weren't exactly fighting with each other to snag me for their mom. They probably all wanted young mothers with smooth skin and breasts not yet decimated by the effects of gravity. Zack looked past the wrinkles and sagging body parts, straight into my soul, and chose me. We are truly a match made in heaven.

This boy, at the age of eight, bedecked his walls with Van

Gogh posters rather than sports pennants. He liked to bake and paint and listen to music. Zack looks at the world with an artist's vision. He is the first of my children to lose his breath at the sight of a vermilion sunset. He is the first to express an interest in seeing Africa and Paris. He says "I love you" with abandon. He even reads. On the third try, I won the boy lottery!

But this year he asked to watch the Super Bowl. How could he do that to me when things were going so well?

Cautiously sweet, he sidled up to Harold and explained, "Dad, I have to watch the Super Bowl. I'll be mocked out of the fourth grade if I don't watch the Super Bowl! I'm a boy!" *Oh God*.

"And Dad, you have to watch it with me and explain what's happening until I understand." *Ohgodohgodohgod*.

Harold can no more explain the Super Bowl than he can share the recipe for the A-bomb. He's neither ashamed nor proud; it's just the way it is. He calmly explained to Zack that he was unable to help him this one time.

That was it. Everything else Harold had done for that boy—the science fair projects, the train set assembly, the chess games, the beach vacations—all were ephemera, because what mattered most now was fitting in with the boys, and Dad was of no use in that particular department of parenting. Propelling the situation from bleak to desperate was the fact that Dan was away at college and Andrew would be watching the game at a party with his friends. Zack was up the proverbial creek.

We needed help. We needed a jock. We needed Jimmy.

Jimmy and his wife, Jo Ann, have been friends of ours for

twenty years. Jimmy knows sports. He has been around athletics all his life and has the well-toned, muscular body to prove it. His son is a college football star. Both Jimmy and his son can recite sports facts as easily as I spew useless Hollywood trivia.

The truth is, Jimmy has also seen more ballet than most men *or* women his age. His beloved daughter, whom he and Jo Ann lost to asthma at the age of nineteen, was an accomplished ballerina, and he delighted in her performances. Jimmy is smart and sweet and selfless, and I couldn't have cared less as I worked myself into a frenzied quest to find a football mentor for my son who was frantic to learn to be a real boy.

Ever the philanthropist, and as expected, Jimmy welcomed the opportunity to aid the athletically challenged. I offered to bring the food and ordered the requisite Super Bowl take-out—chicken wings, hoagies, and chips. I expected the full ambience—crotch-scratching, booing, cheering, and lots of beer. I should have known better.

Jimmy and Zack sat side-by-side on the sofa. Sara, Jimmy and Jo Ann's five-year-old daughter, sat on Jimmy's lap. During the game he stroked her hair and told her jokes and tickled her feet. Wait a minute . . . DURING THE GAME? Wasn't he supposed to tell her to get out of the way because she was obstructing his view? Wasn't Jo Ann supposed to keep her occupied with the women? Jimmy offered Harold a beer and then took two sips of a miniature beer for himself and discarded the rest. He doesn't drink much and never has. Not even when his team is being slaughtered. He does help serve the food, however, and he helps clean up, and he doesn't scratch his nose, much less his privates. I knew that. I KNEW THAT! But this was the Super Bowl! Jimmy explained the whole game to Zack and then they talked about art.

When we left, Zack had become much more than a real boy. He had taken a few giant steps toward becoming a real man.

One wonderful thing about having sons is that they take you into territory you would never explore alone. They take you into a world of men, and what you find there, often to your own surprise, are individuals with all the quirks and questions that make life down here so very rich. The free-thinking, liberal, educated, and nonjudgmental woman that I am, had not only stereotyped men as a gender, but had done so to my own sons—two jocks and an artist. My boys are so much more than either of those things.

My oldest son stopped to help a stranded motorist change a tire a few months ago. The middle one appreciates good jazz and took me to lunch on my birthday. They are both kind and funny and respectful of women. The little one paints and writes and also likes to make a lot of noise. He loves macaroni and cheese and a really good bathroom joke, and he is as real a boy as a boy can be.

I hope the three curly-haired daughters I ordered are out there teaching their father a thing or two about his own expectations of girls. And I hope he has a friend like Jimmy who could help him out by explaining the ballet.

The Sperm Versus the Egg

Sarah Harrison

ACCORDING TO A FRIEND of mine, the difference between boys and girls is that boys are more interested in motion—watching things move as well as moving themselves. "Look at the sperm," she says. "They're so frantic, while the egg rolls peacefully along."

I thought of this seemingly preposterous notion one day as my sons and I drove to piano lessons. They are always happy to go to piano, not because of their great love of music or their astounding musical ability. Nor because of their teacher, a charming seventy-year-old woman, fusses over them shamelessly, although this is certainly nice. The real attraction is the broken hose nozzle in the front yard, which they race toward like magnets for a weekly game of laser beam warrior or something. They've also discovered a fire ant hill the size of Rhode Island. They shake their soda cans over the center of the ant hill and, giggling out of control, pop the tops and fizz the ant hill, the driveway, the trees, and themselves.

Given this fascination, it makes no difference what you decide in your family about guns. Any sticklike thing can become a weapon: those charming wands with glitter in them, musical instruments, that wooden choo-choo Grandpa made, even vacuum cleaner attachment parts. My old Barbie doll wound up in their bucket of bath toys, and one evening when they were getting ready for bed, I heard an earnest "bang, bang, bang!" There they all were, one boy holding bare-naked Barbie by her legs, her upper body pointed forward at a ninety-degree angle, the other two defending themselves with Nerf toys and running around the bathroom.

"Yes, but you have nice boys," people tell me. Nice, maybe; it is true they are more focused than the stereotypical leap-from-the-car, play-every-sport, make-trouble-in-class American boy. One loves to read, one likes to draw, and the other one is into drama, and sometimes—like when they're lying across one of their beds, feet in the air, discussing dinaosaurs or examining a fossil—they look like an idyllic painting. In fact, sometimes I wonder if they're not too calm.

But going across a field or a parking lot, they look like three pinballs lost in la-la land. If one of them sees something like a discarded, bent, rusted bicycle wheel, he stops suddenly, picks it up, and says, "Hey, look at this!" The other two run over, say, "Awesome!" and they kick it, roll it, hit it with whatever sticklike thing is on hand, then finally toss it aside (usually into the path of a pedestrian), and run off in another direction. They glide through those movements together as if following a script with stage directions included.

There seem to be other unwritten male rituals as well, as if some inner voice is constantly saying:

1. Wet towels should be placed on the bathroom floor, balled up, and stepped on—preferably with dirty shoes.

2. Shoes belong on the bed. The covers should be kicked back to expose the sheets so that the sand from the schoolyard and the dried mud from the backyard can keep you company through the night.

3. Do not cultivate a personal relationship with a trash can or recycling bin; your mom should act as go-between. That way, you'll never find yourself standing at the end of the driveway on garbage days like your mom, looking frantically through the can for that lost library book or note home as the sound of the garbage truck brakes grow louder.

4. Lost things can be found by merely raking your forearm across your desk or kicking, soccer-style, at the pile under your bed. In addition, empty jars of mayonnaise and jam should be returned to the fridge.

5. When you come home from somewhere, all lights, computers, video games, and TVs should be turned on and left that way.

6. Many things your mom buys at the grocery store—catsup, shampoo, toothpaste—come with tops. These are unnecessary nuisances and should be left wherever they happen to land. In the case of toothpaste, the mounds that

collect on the counter make good finger paint for writing notes to your brothers on the mirror.

7. Toilets. No instruction needed. When you mom says something like, "That trash can isn't there for you to pee all over," just look up at her and smile.

8. Never, ever, ever, under any circumstances, no matter how much you are nicely asked or forcefully told, put anything back where you found it. The problem is that your mom is operating under the misconception that things belong in certain places.

9. And always love your mom, because she knows the most chocolate-y delicious brand of chocolate-chip cookies and buys them for you, or maybe she even makes her own. And sometimes, she'll sit and watch the NFL draft with you while you eat them.

Perhaps the most important thing moms can do, especially when their sons don't have sisters, is to let them see how things look through girls' eyes—to prove that girls are really very normal creatures. Of course, we've discussed how it takes two to make a baby, but beyond that, I try not to let them draw me in to discussions wherein we all make fun of or complain about the *girls*. Like driving home from school the other day . . .

"How was your day? Did anything eventful happen?"

"Guess what the girls were doing today? *(giggle)* They were walking their dogs at recess."

"Really? Well, that's nice that the school lets people bring their dogs. You mean more than one person had a dog at school?"

"Not real dogs," his brother pipes in over more giggling. "Stuffed animals that look like the dogs from that movie."

"Wait a minute," I say. "You mean, the girls were walking stuffed animals around the playground? On leashes?"

The backseat is now overtaken completely with laughter, but one of the boys manages to eke out, "Light blue ones. With shimmery buckles."

"Oh my," I say, because I am speechless and can think of nothing more to explain away the strange behavior of these alien creatures of the opposite sex. And suddenly, toothpaste mounds on counters and sheets full of sand make perfect sense to me, and I'm glad to have my trio of boys.

The Doll

Amy Oscar

"MOMMY," MY FIVE-YEAR-OLD son said softly. "This is the most beautiful girl I've ever seen." The American Girls catalog was on his lap, open to page Samantha. "I want her."

"Why?" I asked. Max had loved to play with dolls when he was younger, but he hadn't shown much interest in them lately.

"I just want to hold her," he said, a simple request.

"She's really expensive."

"That's okay," Max said, petting the shiny surface of the page.

"Why don't we get you another doll?" I suggested. "There are lots of dolls who are just as beautiful."

"I don't think we'll be able to find one this beautiful." He sighed. "But if we do, I guess it would be okay."

That night when I read him his bedtime stories, I noticed

he had the catalog with him in bed. "I wanted her to be next to me," he explained. "I like to look at her face."

Max had fallen in love. I'd thought we'd have eight, maybe ten, years before we'd see this level of devotion to a girl. I tucked him (and the catalog) in, brewed a really hot cup of tea, and sat down to worry. The price of that doll—eighty dollars—was obscenely high, no matter how beautiful my son might have thought she was. And I thought, once the subject has been opened, his sister's going to want one, too. Finally, there was the little problem of my husband.

"A doll?" Matthew said. "But he's a boy!"

"He says he wants it."

"Get him something else. A train. A basketball. He's a boy!"

"He's sleeping with the catalog. He wants the doll."

"Why?" he asked.

Poor thing, I thought. *He really looks worried.* And sympathetic wife that I am, I said, "Why not?"

My husband threw up his hands. I knew what he was thinking. A lot of people think that way. That dolls turn boys into sissies, the kind of boys who get pushed around on playgrounds. The kind of boys that don't get picked for teams. The kind who might grow up to be—*oh heavens!*—feminine!

I told my husband that playing with dolls might help our son deepen his ability to love and nurture, might let him know that it's okay with us if he is kind, if he wants to take care of someone. I thought these skills might help him be a good father. He might, I told my husband, even gain some fine motor skills buttoning those little buttons and buckling those small shoes. But he was *very* skeptical.

My mother-in-law objected, too. "What a waste of money," she said. "He won't play with it. He'll be off to Little League before it's out of the wrapping paper!"

"Save the box," my sister-in-law counseled. "At least when he forgets about it, you'll have a collector's item."

But finally, I decided to get him the doll. I told him that if he was willing to forgo the usual heap of holiday presents for this one expensive gift, we'd try it. On paper, it looked like it might even cost less this way.

Max received Samantha with great dignity, lifting her gently into his arms. He held her on his lap for a long time, his eyes glowing with pride. At dinner, he set her a place beside him.

My husband gave him a basketball to offset the doll thing, and Max really liked it. But even my husband had to smile (I caught him) at the way Max was loving that doll. And Max *did* play with her. For about a year, he undressed her, put on her little nightgown, and settled her into bed almost every night. In the morning, he woke her up, combed her hair, and dressed her again, his little fingers carefully buttoning her clothes and lacing up her shoes.

But then, when it was time for Max to start kindergarten, he and his sister Katie had a meeting.

"Katie," he said. "You may play with Samantha while I am at school. But when I get home, I want her to look the way she looks in the magazine." Soon after that Max stopped playing with Samantha in favor of his new Power Rangers Megazord. And a few months after that, he "gave" her to Katie. But even though Samantha was officially hers now, every afternoon when Max was due to arrive home on the bus, Katie made sure to return Samantha to her original dress and asked me to re-style her hair. "Max likes her to be the same when he gets home," she reminded me. I didn't think he'd notice.

"Do you still like your Samantha doll?" I asked him one day, as we drove to the mall.

"Yes," he said. "But she's Katie's now."

"Do you play with her?"

"Sometimes." We drove along quietly. I was trying to think of a really good question, one that would get him talking about it so I would have a good ending for this story. Then he said, "Mom, just one thing." (He actually said that.) "When any of my friends who are boys come over, I want you to hide Samantha."

"Why?"

"Because boys have dolls, but they are only allowed to have boy dolls. Samantha is a girl. They wouldn't understand."

"Ah," I said, thinking: *But I understand. I really do.*

Max is nine now, and he doesn't play with dolls anymore. He loves baseball, and this year, he begged us for a basketball hoop. He's a regular kid. A "real" boy doing real boy things with one added feature: He's really nice.

And though I don't know whether or not the doll had anything to do with that, I'm really glad he got it.

Snakes and Snails

Candy Chand

I WOULDN'T HAVE IT any other way. Sugar and spice and everything nice was all I could think about during my first pregnancy. Other more experienced moms insisted on performing their hocus pocus: "You're having a boy. I can tell by the way you're carrying it . . . by the way this thread and charm move back and forth across your belly . . . the fact that you're craving strawberries and not apples . . ." and on and on. But I promptly dismissed each of their misguided notions; I was determined to have a girl.

Soon enough, however, hard-core science replaced old wives tales when my doctor pronounced, "Your ultrasound shows you're having a boy."

Nope. No way. Save your scientific evidence—it made no difference to me. I dug my heels in even deeper and declared to everyone who'd listen that I was having a girl. When my daughter Tiffany was born in November, I smugly—and lovingly—wrapped her in one of the many soft pink blankets I had bought during my pregnancy. Our mother-daughter bond was immediate and profound.

Six years later, I was pregnant again. Still just as determined, still ignoring other people's firm predictions of a baby boy, I was sure I'd have another girl. I knew in my heart that it shouldn't matter. I knew the right thing to say was, "as long as the baby is healthy, the sex doesn't matter," but it did. Guilty as it made me feel, I simply did not want a boy.

One friend tried to console me with what she thought was a precious little boy moment. "My son likes to bring me presents," she said smiling, "you know, things from the garden like freshly dug worms—warm from the earth and still wiggling—and plops them in my lap." She giggled with delight like she was talking about a lover bringing her a box of chocolates! *Gee great,* I thought. *Spare me the details, please.*

And then it hit me. I was walking through a grocery store with my husband one day, and I stopped dead in my tracks. "Okay," I said. "I have a confession to make. I'm going to tell you why this baby just has to be a girl." Looking a bit concerned, my husband braced himself for what I might say. To tell you the truth, I braced *myself* for what I might say, because I wasn't really sure where this sudden revelation was coming from. I just knew it needed to come out before I exploded.

"I've never had a brother, never even had a close male friend." There, I said it. "I don't know anything about boys. I don't *do* sports and guns and trucks . . . and worms!" It was bubbling forth now, all my fear and anxiety—right there in the dairy section. "What's more, I'm afraid I might not bond with a son. What if I treat him like I'm only his baby-sitter? What if I pat him on the head gently, speak politely to him, and make his favorite treats but never really fall in love? Our baby just has to be a girl—it wouldn't be fair to the child any other way."

My husband tried to calm me down and reassure me. "You'll be a great mom to a boy, honey. You'll see—you'll bond with this baby no matter what. Just relax and have faith." Despite his optimism, I wasn't convinced. Then he put his arms around me and said, "After all, I'm a boy and you fell in love with me, didn't you?"

"Labor day" arrived just a few weeks later, and as we drove to the hospital, I prayed that my husband was right. When the baby finally came, the doctor held him up for me to see and proudly announced, "A beautiful baby boy!" And it was immediate: My heart exploded with unimaginable love and the connection was unmistakable. I knew at that very moment I'd never feel like just a baby-sitter to this child—no polite words or stiff pats on the head with this little love of my life! And nine years later, Nicholas and I have a mother-son bond more wonderful than I ever thought possible. Snakes and snails and puppy-dog tails? Piece of cake!

Of Whiskers and Cowlicks

Melanie J. Grimes

I WATCHED MY SON shave this morning as we talked about him leaving for college. He leaves in two weeks. I asked him if he needs me to buy him a razor or is he planning on continuing to borrow his daddy's—you know, fly home every morning before school. He doesn't know. This is too complicated a question for him and too far in the distance for him to worry about.

It reminds me of a time he was five and picking up mealy apples from an old apple tree. He'd pick an apple and carry it over to his plastic pail on the porch by the house. Then he'd walk back to the tree, get another apple, and repeat the process, one by one. A neighbor girl came over. She carried her pail to the spot below the apple tree and sat there, plopping her apples into her pail, without hardly taking a step. My son watched her for a while, and then decided she had a good idea and copied her.

Boys have a strange logic. They are deliciously simple and unassuming. They are egalitarian, including each other in their animal pack as long as the pecking order isn't drastically disrupted. Any two boys, given a ball and a mitt or hoop, can entertain each other for hours, regardless of age. But they cannot pick apples.

When my daughters were developing sophistication and breasts, my son and his buddies were lying on their backs in the snow making weird noises. Wherever they were, they made weird noises. They still do. They're self-conscious in a different way, I realize. When my son decides to find out how he looks talking into a new cell phone, he gazes intently at the mirror while pretending to talk, until he's satisfied the phone stance is cool enough.

But he's not self-conscious about shaving. He does it by male animal instinct. I'm not sure why he shaves. He does a bad job, running his father's razor over the darkest spots, his sideburns and under his nose, until the shadows are gone and he's satisfied. Getting the cowlick to lay down on the back of his head takes a little longer—some water (it used to be spit) and some head slapping—until it lays flat for the two seconds he's watching it in the mirror. He doesn't see the hair spring back up—Alfalfa-like—as he turns away and walks out of the bathroom. He has two cowlicks, actually—one going clockwise and the other counterclockwise. When he was a baby, the hair between these maelstroms would stand up on end on top of his head. "Someday," I'd mumble to myself, "this is going to drive him crazy."

"Mom, remember when you used to say that someday this was going to drive me crazy?" he said when he was sixteen. "Well, today is that day." He has yet to win the cowlick battle.

He is leaving for college in two weeks, cowlicks and all, and not a razor to his name. I worry about him.

Who will remind him of all the things I nag him about now? Who will remember what his cowlick was like when he was a baby and the best way to train it down? And who will love him in spite of the hair sticking up on the back of his head? Who will appreciate his complexity, his simplicity, and his innocent beauty and adapt their life to his nuances the way I have? Who will sense his every mood? How will he cope on his own? And who will buy him a razor when he suddenly figures out his dad's isn't by the sink?

Maybe the same girl who showed him how to pick apples.

PART FOUR

Blessings

"A boy is Truth with dirt on its face, Beauty with a cut on its finger, Wisdom with bubble gum in its hair, and the Hope of the future with a frog in its pocket."

—Alan Marshall Beck

Puppy Love

Ron Brand

CHRISTMAS MORNING WAS a special one that year for my two little boys, Kenny, six and Jeff, two. Amidst the packages under the tree was a new little puppy with a big red bow around its neck. He didn't sit there as still as a stuffed animal would have when the boys ran in to see what Santa had left. Instead, he scampered over the other packages, wagging his little tail at the sight of his new owners.

The puppy was a mix between a poodle and a terrier, with short curly champagne blonde hair, and the boys fell instantly in love with their new playmate. Fortunately, we had a large yard in our new, roomy southern California home so "Corky"—the name Kenny immediately pronounced on him—was living a good, active puppy life. He was quickly housebroken and was such a cute little rascal that we all enjoyed him immensely.

It was 1965 and I was a professional baseball player at the time, so when spring came, our family was forced to move to Houston, Texas, where I played for the Astros. We would be spending the spring and summer months there. We packed our things, closed up the house, and headed southeast to Houston. The trip took two days, and, thankfully, Corky and the boys slept most of the trip. When we finally arrived, we moved into a small, two-bedroom furnished apartment which would be our temporary home—complete with the ever-popular '60s green shag rugs.

There was one drawback: There was no yard for Corky to play in at the apartment complex, and the indoor space was much more limited than in our California home. But we'd make the best of it—it was only for six months, after all. Not long after we got our things unpacked and settled, though, Corky began to chew on things. He chewed the newspaper, he chewed the corners of the furniture, he chewed the table legs, the drapes, and anything he could get his mouth around. We tried everything to break him of the habit. We bought him chew toys, took him out for walks, paid lots of attention to him, and played with him, but nothing seemed to work for any length of time. And this was *not* our furniture.

One night I returned home from a road trip in the wee hours of the morning. As I turned on the light to get a snack, I noticed a large hole in the carpet—a hole that went all the way through to the cement slab. Corky had really done it this time! I went in and woke my wife, who was flabbergasted because the hole hadn't been there when she went to bed. We talked about our options and finally decided that we should try to find Corky a home with another family who had a yard.

I knew how difficult this would be for the boys, especially Kenny, but heck, it was hard for me, too. I hated when I had to leave my family to go on the road, and I somehow felt that this little puppy helped make up for my absences. But something had to be done about our family's latest addition, so I decided to approach Kenny with simple logic, man to man.

The next morning, we called Kenny in and showed him all the damage his puppy had done. We explained that Corky must've been very frustrated and confused with his new cramped quarters and that we should think about what would be the best environment for the puppy—what would make *him* the happiest. Kenny nodded his head, probably not having any clue where this line of logic was going. When we finally told him that it would be best to find a new home and family for Corky where he wouldn't get into so much trouble, Kenny's lip started quivering and his big blue eyes filled with tears. Trying not to let us see the tear running down his cheek, he looked straight at the floor and quietly agreed that we should do whatever would make his puppy happiest.

That afternoon, my wife and I were in the bedroom reading the paper and talking about the news on the baseball front and about the kids' activities while I was away. From the living room, we heard Kenny's voice, sobbing and saying, "Good-bye, Corky. I hope you'll remember me because I'll never forget you . . . good-bye . . . I hope you'll be good for your next owner, and I hope they have a big yard so you won't get in any more chewing trouble . . . but if you don't like it, Corky . . . you know I'll come and find you . . ."

We sat there, heartbroken, as Kenny bravely tried to explain to Corky how it would cost his mom and dad too much money to fix up the apartment if he kept chewing things up. My wife and I looked at each other and without even a word between us, we called Kenny into our room to try to comfort him. And then I heard myself saying that maybe there was one more thing we could try to help Corky overcome his chewing. "Let's have a special family prayer," I continued, "and ask God to help Corky stop chewing."

As the four of us knelt down and held hands, Kenny said the prayer for his puppy. Over and over, he expressed how much he loved Corky and wanted him to stay with our family and could God please help him stop chewing because it wasn't really fair to have to give up a member of your family just because of his teeth. Throughout the day, Kenny would hold Corky, telling him how much he loved him and that he just knew God was going to help him get over his bad habit.

As I watched, I ached for Kenny. No baseball losing streak or slump could be as painful as what he was going through that day. But what hurt most was thinking about how Kenny would handle it when Corky didn't magically change overnight. Yes, I believed in prayer, but I considered it primarily a source of comfort and strength to Kenny in his difficult time, not as an instant cure.

Trying to distract myself from my anguish, I started working. I fixed the hole in the shag and sanded and stained all the chew marks on the damaged furniture. By the end of the day, there was not a shred of evidence of Corky's misdeeds.

* * *

What is it about the faith of a child? What miracles can happen between a boy and his beloved dog? And why do we question the wisdom of those who, ages ago, taught, "and a little child shall lead them." From that day forward, Corky never chewed on anything. He never showed the slightest inclination to do so ever again—not even with the newspaper. Kenny's faith and love had been rewarded, and Corky became a permanent member of our family, regardless of where we lived.

Kenny's parents learned a powerful lesson: When a child utters a simple prayer and believes with all his heart, God will pour forth great blessings. And those of us lucky enough to be in the vicinity can receive just a sprinkling of residual blessings, too. For me that year, I received no greater gift than to watch my sweet, believing son play with a very happy and loyal puppy.

Our Little Piece of Heaven

Teri Brinsley

SINCE THE DAY he started babbling, I have known that my son, Nicolas, had a strong spiritual side. Before he could even talk, he would communicate with "baby talk" and by pointing, as most toddlers do. He was such an unusually happy baby that I felt he was somehow blessed with a keen sense of love and God. People have been drawn to him since the day he was born, often commenting on his heartwarming smile or his cheerful demeanor. They often say, "There's just something about him . . ." and it's true. Because of that something, I believe, Nicolas recently saved my life.

First, let me tell you a little more about my son's unusual gift. When Nicolas was about sixteen months old, I playfully asked him where Jesus lived. I didn't expect much of a response; I was just curious what he would say. Maybe if he was really in tune, I thought, he would point to the sky. He astonished me when he immediately answered my question by pointing to his heart and smiling. I wondered who had taught him that cute trick, but after asking all who knew him, I realized he had thought of the connection on his own.

There were other times, as a toddler, that he would be playing alone with his toys. Then suddenly I would hear him start to giggle. On more than one occasion, I would look to see what he was laughing at, only to find him staring and laughing at nothing other than our empty hallway or the center of a room. I would ask, "Why are you giggling, Nicolas?" He'd look up at me and say, "the angel," and then turn right back to what he could see that I couldn't. On other occasions, we'd be sitting on the couch together and he'd start laughing. When I would ask him what was so funny, his reply would be, simply, "Oh, it was just God. He was tickling me again." Nicolas does seem to have a special connection, and it came in very handy that Saturday afternoon last summer.

My husband, David, and Nicolas were running errands around town that day about four o'clock, while I treated myself to a manicure and pedicure at a local salon. As David drove down the road, Nicolas was happily singing to one of his favorite CDs when suddenly, he stopped and his face filled with concern. "Is something bad going to happen today, Daddy?" he said in a worried voice. David was startled by the question, thinking he must not have heard him correctly. "What did you say, Nicolas?" he asked. Nicolas became even more concerned.

"Change the music," he said with urgency in his voice.

Nicolas's whole demeanor had changed; he didn't want to sing or laugh but was suddenly deeply disturbed. Sensing something was truly wrong, my husband pulled the car to the side of the road. He glanced at the clock, which read 4:20, and then turned and faced Nicolas in the backseat.

"Nicolas, are you worried about something?" he asked.

"Something bad is going to happen," Nicolas responded. His original question was now fact. David listened and then asked, "What do you think we should do? Do you want to pray?"

Nicolas quickly and emphatically replied, "Yes! We need to pray!" So there on the side of the road my husband and son prayed that God would send his guardian angels to protect our family that day so nothing bad would happen. When they had said their "amens," Nicolas brightened up and said, "Please turn the music back on, Daddy." And they drove on, the gloomy weight having been lifted off their shoulders.

Oblivious to all this, I was enjoying being pampered at the salon. My nails were close to being finished, and my feet were soaking in a warm, sudsy bath in a tub below me. I glanced at the clock, which read 4:30. As the nail technician put the final touches on my nails, she reached across and turned on the fan that sat at the corner of her table to help my nails dry. Another manicurist sat near my feet, getting ready to pull them from the water. Realizing she had forgotten the towels, she jumped up and headed for the cabinet. In her hurry, she didn't see that the cord to the fan had gotten caught around her ankle. In one split-second yank, the humming fan flew from the corner of the table, hurling with great force right for the tub of water my feet were in. It happened so suddenly, I didn't have time to think.

But for some reason I can't explain, the instant before it hit the water, a tiny part of its base hit the side of the tub, bouncing the entire fan up and away from the water and onto the floor. I sat there staring at my feet in the water and the fan still running on the floor next to the tub. I was stunned. The fact that I had almost been electrocuted was sinking in, and the thought made me queasy.

"You *do* realize what almost just happened to you, don't you?" a woman sitting near me said, her face pale from what she had just witnessed.

"Yes," I replied weakly, in shock. "I must have a guardian angel who knocked the fan out of the way just in time. I don't understand how it could've kept from falling in otherwise." I said a prayer of thanks for the protection and as I was silently praying, the electrical fuse blew and the entire salon's power went out. Knowing that the outage would've naturally occurred had the fan fallen into the water, I felt a confirmation that something supernatural had indeed happened and I thanked God again for his guardian angels.

Leaving the salon about 4:45, I called my husband on my cell phone. Still shaken, I explained what had just happened and then David told me about what had transpired in the car with Nicolas. After we compared notes, it was clear that our son, Nicolas, had been right: Something bad *was* going to happen that day but because of his keen—and divine—intuition, we believe he prevented a horrible accident and saved my life.

It's not unusual to hear phrases like "thank heaven" and

"count your blessings" in casual conversation today, but we take those words quite literally in our family. We are both thankful for and blessed by our little boy, Nicolas. He's our own piece of heaven here on earth.

A Very Special Christmas Stocking

Anne Frazier

THE YEAR HAD BEEN a good one for our little family. Now, as the year was drawing quickly to a close, we were busy preparing for the approaching Christmas season.

One evening a few days before Christmas, I had gone shopping and was just unlocking our front door when I heard the phone ringing. I was tempted to just let it ring, but instead I rushed in to answer it. To my surprise, I learned that a long-awaited blessing was about to come into our lives—a baby born that morning was available for adoption. The newborn boy had had a stressful gestation period and was currently substance-addicted.

"He's strong, and he's a fighter. I think with a lot of care and love he will make it just fine," the man arranging the adoption told me over the phone. "We'll need to keep him at the hospital for a while, but now that he has a home to go to, we'll get him there as quickly as we can. We'll get him ready, and you get ready for him."

Although we were thrilled, my husband and I decided not to tell anyone about the baby because of the uncertainty of his health. But we began to prepare for his arrival and because we had adopted before, we knew the procedure to be certified as adoptive parents.

The next few days flew by as we got ready for the holidays and a new baby. We mentioned to the children that we might get a very special present for Christmas; some guessed it was a new car, others hoped for a dog. No one guessed it would be a baby brother.

Along with the other preparations, we also spent time planning for an evening of Christmas caroling, Christmas readings, and holiday refreshments at our home for some neighbors and friends from church. On Christmas Eve morning, all was ready for our family's Christmas, the get-together with our friends, and our new son's arrival. Sure enough, the phone rang about noon. "Merry Christmas!" our doctor friend exclaimed. "He's yours today!"

Quickly we gathered together the little bundle of new baby clothes, called a family friend to stay with the children, then left for the hospital, telling the children we were going after the special gift. When we arrived, the nursery staff took us in to see our new son.

He was thin and had big, bright blue eyes and dark hair. The nurses shed a few tears as they taught me how to take care of their "Christmas boy." Sensing their attachment to the tiny baby they had cared for, I gave them the bundle of clothing and said I'd wait outside while they dressed him and told him good-bye. In a few minutes, they came out with the baby, who was wrapped in an oversized red Christmas stocking. Though it would take many months to complete his adoption, from that very moment, we knew that baby was ours.

For the next hour, my husband and I drove around, marveling at the magic of the season and the joy of adding this child to our family. Late in the afternoon we arrived home, bearing our wondrous Christmas gift—our baby boy. The children were elated. Suddenly it seemed like Christmas, really Christmas—a time for celebrating a new baby and the miracle of his birth.

The day passed quickly. Almost before we realized it, we could hear our friends approaching, their rich voices ringing out their joy as they walked up to the house singing Christmas carols. I had placed our new baby boy in a basket in the center of a table in the living room of our home. As the happy people filed into the room, their voices became subdued as they realized the presence of this "little stranger."

Within a few moments, there was total silence in the room as they all looked upon the sleeping newborn child. Then softly, and together, they began to sing, "Silent night! Holy night!" And after they finished they all stood in silence. With tears streaming down his face, one of the men said, "The magic of this moment is too beautiful for words."

A warmth filled the room, and our new little stranger's unexpected presence filled every heart with thoughts of another baby boy born on a Christmas long ago.

Lunch Money Miracle

Linda Doty

"SHE'S TOO STRICT. She won't even let us turn in a paper with a bent corner!" Chad whined. It was his first day of sixth grade, and he was already begging me to get him into another class with a different teacher. Mrs. Kelly was a new teacher at the school and I didn't know anything about her, but I stood firm. I'd seen it happen before: She'd probably end up being his favorite teacher and he just might learn a thing or two from her in the process. The year progressed as I suspected, and Mrs. Kelly grew to earn the kids' respect and win their hearts as well.

That year was one of growth for our entire family. My husband had lost his business, and we were forced to start over financially. With six children and a new home, money was tight and we felt the squeeze. As parents, we struggled with just how much to share with the kids, ages three to eighteen. We didn't want to burden them with our problems or destroy their sense of security, but we also felt they needed to know there wouldn't be lots of money for "extras" that year. The older children were concerned and did what they could to help and the younger children breezed through the year unaffected. Chad was right in the middle, at a very vulnerable and sensitive age. Never one to voice his need for things like new clothes or shoes, he'd often go without longer than the other kids if I didn't keep close tabs on him.

One small strain on the budget was the daily need for five school lunches, which somehow seemed cheaper to buy at school than purchasing all the supplies at the grocery store. Money was put in a cup on a shelf in the kitchen at the beginning of each week, and the kids took out their portion each morning on the way to school. At the end of the first week, I noticed a few dollars left over in the cup and I assumed I'd counted wrong. As the weeks progressed, though, there was consistently several dollars in the cup each Friday. Naturally, I didn't want any of the children to go hungry, so I asked them if they were each taking their share and they assured me they were. Something told me to focus in on Chad, but sure enough, I watched him take his lunch money out of the cup each day with the rest of the kids.

It was later in the school year when I was having a regular parent-teacher conference with Chad's teacher that I learned the truth about Chad. With great caution, Mrs. Kelly shared with me the fact that she had noticed him not eating any lunch on many school days at the beginning of the year. After a little gentle prodding, Chad had tearfully admitted to her his worries about his family's financial situation, adding that skipping lunch was the only way he could think of to help. He confided to his teacher that he'd take the money out of the cup every morning when he knew his mother was watching and then put it back when she'd leave the room. He had done this several days a week for months.

It turns out that Mrs. Kelly had not only taught her students the important lessons of reading, writing, and arithmetic that year, but also invaluable lessons about love and sacrifice and mutual respect. She was so impressed by Chad's sensitivity and desire to help his family that she had struck a deal with him. She would make a sandwich for him every day and put it in his desk without anyone else knowing, so Chad could continue contributing in secret to his family's funds. She had done this for the better part of the year.

Initially, I was embarrassed and humiliated that Chad's teacher was aware of our financial struggles and upset that he would share such confidences. At the same time, I was deeply touched and humbled by her sincere love and concern. Mrs. Kelly made it very clear that this had been a pact between her and Chad and that she hoped I would allow him to continue his genuine and anonymous sacrifice for his family.

Eventually, our financial situation improved, but I think my middle son grew up in the process that year. There was a new sense of pride about Chad, a certain confidence in his demeanor; I think he felt that his contribution was important and that he could make a difference—at home, at school, or in his sports. I never again watched him take or put money back into the cup, and it wasn't until the next summer that I told him about my conversation with Mrs. Kelly. But at the end of each week during that school year, I'd tenderly pick up those extra dollars left in the cup and think about what one unselfish son had taught me about real love and sacrifice.

Sleep with Your Angels

Jaymie Reeber Kosa

LAST SUMMER, MY TWO-YEAR-OLD, Trevor, spent his first extended vacation with my best friend, her two children, and myself at her beach house in New York. Our husbands' schedules weren't compatible, but we decided it would be great fun to spend quality time together with the children.

Each day proved to be exhausting with swimming in the pool, visits to the local library, walks to the local duck pond, and of course, jaunts on the beach. The kids were able to pick fresh blueberries, play make-believe, and jump out all their energy on a big trampoline. Her home was an inviting and exciting place to be for a child or an adult, and Trevor got along quite nicely with her children, Hannah, four, and Henry, two. Yet there was a serious problem I had to deal with every day—bedtime.

Trevor would not fall asleep alone in the room we shared together. He would cry and fuss unless I sat in the room with him until he could no longer keep his eyes open. Even when I thought it was safe to leave, he would wake up later, notice I wasn't there, and begin to cry. Each night he became very anxious about going to bed as I tried to find ways to help ease his fears. Warm baths, lullabies, and stories were failing me, and I was becoming exasperated. Then Charlotte taught me a lovely idea.

Every night, I'd hear her put her kids to sleep, and just before she shut the door, she'd whisper, "Sleep with your angels." And, though her children were more accustomed to overnight visits at the beach house, they always slept soundly and peacefully. That evening, after his warm bath and several stories, Trevor began fussing about going to sleep. So I put him on my lap and told him I had a magical secret to share with him. I whispered in my softest voice, "Have you ever heard of an angel?"

"No, Mommy," he whispered back.

Then I cradled him, looked deep into his blue eyes, and said, "Do you know there are angels who love you, guide you, and protect you all the time? And all you have to do is call on those angels when you get a bit scared, and they'll be there in an instant when you need them? Now, tonight, I know you might be a little scared, but I want you to call out to your angels if you feel frightened at all. Okay, honey?" I asked.

"Okay, Mommy," he whispered.

Then, I rocked him while we sang silly songs about his toes and giggled together. After our goodnight hugs and kisses, I placed him in his bed and said, "Sleep with the angels." When I walked out of the room, there was silence.

Of course, about five minutes later he began to cry, but I quietly walked in and told him to call on his angels to protect him and then he was quiet for the night. The rest of the vacation was wonderfully calm, except for a few "it's mine" power struggles between the two boys. Bedtime eventually became a peaceful ritual where all the kids would take a bath and read stories together. Then, Hannah and Henry would jump into their beds, and Trevor and I would travel down the hall, cuddle a bit, read a few more stories, then dim the lights. Each night I'd whisper, "Sleep with your angels," and Trevor would playfully call back, "Thank you, Mommy . . . you, too, Mommy."

One morning several months later, he shared a magical secret with me. It was quite early, around 7 A.M., but the sun was shining, and I could hear Trevor talking in his room. He sounded like he was talking to someone, but the words were muffled, so I quietly snuck down the hallway to see if I could hear better. Unfortunately, our floor was squeaky, so he heard my footsteps and immediately began to call out, "Who's there?" We played a silly guessing game while I hid outside his bedroom door before I came in with my morning hugs and kisses.

"Trevor, were you talking to your angels this morning?"

"Yes, Mommy," he said.

"Oh, really. Would you tell me about them?"

This was a moment I had thought about for a long time, because I truly believed in angels, spirits, and guides. I had also read many stories about children and their innate ability to be in touch with the spiritual world because of their implicit faith and lack of skepticism about angels. Trevor, however, answered my question with a puzzling gaze, so I decided to try another approach.

"Trev, how many angels do you have?"

"Two, Mommy."

"Wow!" I said. "That is wonderful. Do they protect you every night?"

"Yeah," he said. "Can I have orange juice?"

"Do you talk with your angels at night?" I asked, ignoring his simple request. I was so intrigued with his comments about angels that I just had to find out more.

"YES!" he said impatiently as he tried to swing his leg over the crib rail. At this point, I became terribly fascinated, so I whispered, "Do your angels have names, Trev?"

"Yeah," he said forlornly as he sat back down on his blue comforter, grabbing his tattered white blanket, and staring at the door.

"Will you tell me their names, honey?" I begged.

Then, he bounced up, put his hands on the crib rail, and leaned toward me. With his silliest grin, he arched his blond eyebrows playfully above his precocious blue eyes and whispered, "Mommy and Daddy."

The Horse with No Name

Kathryn A. Beres

SATURDAY HAD FINALLY ARRIVED, and Mitchell was anxious to get going to the local auction. Every third weekend of the month, potential buyers came from all over the state to the small town in Wisconsin where we live, with great anticipation about being the highest bidder on things like horses, livestock, or even farm machinery. This particular Saturday, my son had saved up enough birthday money added to his accumulated monthly chore allowance to hopefully purchase a used but sturdy western saddle at the auction. With money to burn, we set off to find a real bargain.

Arriving at the auction grounds, my son set out to examine each and every saddle mounted on the display racks for observation. After careful and intense scrutiny, one saddle caught his eye. Its dark brown leather and dull silver tooling made it appear very "broken in," to say the least. Though it lacked sparkle and instant appeal, it had potential and was the perfect size for Mitchell. Not knowing where the bidding price would begin, my little fellow tightly clutched his hard earned "saddle fund" of one-hundred-fifty-seven dollars, hoping to become the final bidder and claim the saddle.

Normally at this auction, all saddle items are brought out for bid first and the horses are reserved to auction off last. For some reason, though, on this particular day the auctioneer decided to bring the horses out for bid before anything else.

As the auction assistants rode or led the horses out one by one, a mass of people gathered around to observe and start bidding on their favorite horse. With his money now folded and tucked deep inside his pocket, Mitchell and I watched the beauty of these majestic animals as they pranced and plodded around the exhibit ring one at a time. For most of the horses, bids opened at eight hundred dollars and climbed to at least twelve hundred dollars. That is, until they brought out Number 343—a scrawny, young Arab Paint horse. This horse had no name, and the assistant had to practically drag him by a lead rope into the ring. As the auctioneer hesitantly opened the bidding at seven hundred dollars, the crowd was silent. The pathetic-looking creature staggered around the ring slowly, hoping somehow to capture the heart of a new owner.

The auctioneer continued to lower the opening bid until, finally, someone in the crowd held up his bidding number at a measly seventy-five dollars. As my son gazed across the mob of people, he recognized the only bidder as the purchaser from the slaughterhouse. Suddenly, he was tugging at my arm, begging me to hold up my card to outbid the man.

"Mom, please!" my son pleaded. "That guy is gonna kill that poor horse! Please can we buy it? Please?" The intent of his heart was plain and simple. He wanted to rescue this lonely, pathetic animal and was even willing to give up his saddle money in order to give it a loving home.

For a brief moment, I actually saw the slightest bit of potential in this pitiful animal, just as I had with the old, broken-down saddle. Suddenly, taken by Mitchell's compassion, I found myself nodding yes to his pleas to make a bid. We left that afternoon not with an old, dark brown saddle, but with a feeble, dispirited young horse. But on the drive back to our farm, I couldn't have been more proud of my son and his newest addition to our family.

It has been four years since that auction. I must admit that I haven't returned to the grounds since that day, being a bit fearful that I might be persuaded to rescue other unfortunate horses, but I'll never regret bringing home the horse with no name.

In the early days after #343's arrival, the vet made numerous trips to our house to treat him. The bills he left behind were usually higher than his hopes for the horse's improvement, many times exceeding the original purchase price itself. But over time and with Mitchell's special formula of TLC, that weary old horse we now call "Chief" has been transformed into a strong, spirited equine. My son continues to compete with him at the 4-H level, achieving his goals and often winning awards. And it remains a mystery—and a miracle—to me, what the love and devotion of one young boy can accomplish.

Daily Bread

Teri Brinsley

I DON'T HAVE TIME *for this!* I said to myself as the waves of nausea swept over me. A busy mother of three who also helped her husband run a business simply didn't have time for "sick leave." As I sat there sipping punch at my nephew's birthday party that warm June afternoon, I wondered how I had caught the flu and hoped it would be gone in twenty-four hours.

But by the first week in July, I was getting concerned because I still wasn't feeling well, although I kept my worries to myself. Just keep going, keep busy, and it'll pass. We were getting ready to go to a Fourth of July barbecue with my husband David's family, and I was busy preparing the food.

I scooped up my youngest son, Zachary, and set him on the kitchen counter as I started packing the supplies. His chubby three-year-old fingers immediately grasped for whatever was within reach, and the first thing he went for was my little ceramic scripture verse-holder shaped like a miniature loaf of bread. Although he was young, Zachary loved to pull out a different card each day and have me read it to him. The side of the little loaf was inscribed with "Our Daily Bread," and I had loved it as a little girl, just like Zachary did now. I always thought the verse my mother would help me read each day was my own personal message from the Almighty, and so my mother passed it on to me when I married so I could share it with my children.

The girls were gathering up beach towels and sunblock, David was packing the car with chairs and blankets, and I was putting the finishing touches on the potato salad. Oblivious to the commotion around him, Zachary sat with his scripture card in hand, chirping in a sing-song voice the same little sound over and over as he "read" from his card. As I turned from the counter to put the salad into a bag, his chanting suddenly became clear. I recognized the word he had been saying over and over, and I froze as it sunk in. "Baby-baby-baby-baby," he repeated quietly as if reading it from the card.

"David, come here!" I yelled. "Listen to your son for a minute!" David came around the corner of the garage, and the two of us stood there listening to Zachary's preaching from the scriptures. I kept thinking he'd move on to another word, but his message was loud and clear. "Hey, Zach," I finally said with a gulp and a weak laugh, "are you saying 'baby'?" He stopped for a moment, looked up at me with a sheepish grin, and without hesitating, nodded his little round head. "Uh-huh."

"Baby," I repeated. "Is someone . . . having a baby?" I

asked. Again Zach smiled and said, "Uh-huh." Now he had our complete attention. Afraid to hear my own words, I quietly said, "Who is having a baby, Zachary?" He looked at me with that knowing grin and replied very simply, "You are."

David, of course, thought it was all a joke and quipped, "Does he know something we don't know?" But I wasn't laughing, and David stopped smiling when I replied, "Well, I haven't been feeling very good for a few weeks now, maybe he does."

Why was my three-year-old saying this? I couldn't really be pregnant—the dates didn't add up when I did the calculations, and we certainly hadn't been planning on this. But just to be sure, I bought a home pregnancy test; that way when I called the doctor in a day or two, he'd have more information to help him figure out what was wrong with me. But as I stood there counting the seconds for the test results, it became plain as day. I walked back into the kitchen and called to David in the garage, "Honey, we need to talk"—the words that make every man shudder. When he walked in, I simply held out the test strip.

Looking back, I smile when I remember my concern over the news that day—both the prospect of being a mother of four and the realization that my little boy had been the bearer of such good tidings. But Zachary has a little brother now named Nicolas, and they're the best of friends.

Nicolas worships his big brother—he thinks Zachary hung the moon in the sky and lit the stars. We know Zach didn't exactly hang the moon, but he definitely has an inside line to heaven.

PART FIVE

Obstacles

"Growing is not the easy, plain sailing business that it is commonly supposed to be; it is hard work, harder than any, but a growing boy can understand."

—Samuel Butler

Great Expectations

Rosemarie Riley

I STILL REMEMBER the time I overheard my parents talking in the kitchen when I was expecting my first child. "The doctor thinks this one will be okay," my mom had said.

Of course the baby will be okay, I told myself. It just had to be. I'd had two miscarriages, and I wasn't getting any younger. Thirty-three was not young to be having my first child, as my mom had reminded me many times over the past seven months.

Although I knew my mother meant well, I began harboring fears about the baby I was carrying. As long as it would be healthy—that's all I cared about. I didn't even want to know whether I was carrying a boy or a girl; that excitement could wait until the delivery room.

Two months later, as I nursed the warm bundle in my

arms, I stared at the small ivory face, the closed eyes, and the wispy auburn hair. Then I counted, one . . . two . . . three . . . My son had ten fingers and toes. At that moment, I was grateful for the blessings bestowed on me. David was perfect!

Over the next three years, he filled my days with giggles, hugs, and kisses. I had never felt such happiness. Then one day, as I looked out the window, I noticed David playing with the children next door. As I continued to watch, the boys placed David in the center of a circle. *How nice,* I thought. Those older boys are really being kind to put up with a three-year-old.

But suddenly my joy turned to disappointment. The boys were starting to tease David—pointing at him and asking him to say their names. I knew what a difficult task that would be for my son; he had developed a stammer over recent months. The harder he tried, the more noticeable and funny his stammer became to the other children. But instead of crying, as I was sure he would in the middle of this group, David giggled. The more the boys teased him, the more he giggled. My heart went out to him, and I knew I had to do something.

The following morning I took David to see Dr. Kendall, the family doctor. For the next fifteen minutes, I watched as he examined David. Finally, Dr. Kendall put his glasses down on the table. "I'm going to refer you to Dr. Smith, a hearing specialist. He'll take it from there." I left the office clutching David's hand, suddenly feeling that my perfect world was beginning to crumble.

As I drove home on the freeway, I tried to ignore the questions that kept gnawing at me. Did David have a hearing problem? If he did, would the problem be permanent? And how would I break the news to my husband?

The next afternoon, I watched nervously as Dr. Smith examined David's ears and asked him a series of questions. As my son struggled to answer, a frown crossed the doctor's face. Finally, Dr. Smith came around to the front of his desk. "Your son has a hearing loss," he said, patting my arm sympathetically. "The scar tissue in the left ear will affect his residual hearing. We'll go ahead and insert Grommet tubes and that should help, but with the hearing loss he has, don't expect too much of him."

Leaving the doctor's office, I felt as though I'd just been handed a life sentence for my son. At that moment, I prayed for the strength to cope with the upcoming operation, but more important, for David to overcome this obstacle.

When we met with the speech therapist, she echoed Dr. Smith's diagnosis. "Remember, David has a hearing loss," she said. "The scar tissue will affect how much he hears. Don't expect too much of him."

Twice a week for the next two years I took David to speech lessons. Over time he improved, but I knew we still had a long way to go before he would feel confident in his speech and hearing.

Each year in elementary school, I made sure the teacher placed David in the front row of class so he wouldn't miss a word; I knew how frustrated he became when he couldn't understand what was being said. "David is managing just fine," the teacher would say at each parent conference, but in my heart I knew it wasn't always true. There were many times when he got angry because he couldn't hear the teacher's instructions or the kids teased him about his stammer. Those were the times he'd come home and burst into tears.

Throughout the years, he and I would sit together and I'd listen to stories about his day and reassure him everything would be all right. At night as I lay in bed, my own words would haunt me. Was I just kidding myself and my young son? Would everything really be all right ever again?

When David began bringing homework home, we'd review the work together and I'd listen to him read, painstakingly sounding out each word. Watching the frustration on his face when he couldn't get it right almost broke my heart and I'd hear the doctor's words echoing once again, "Don't expect too much from him."

In junior high, David's stammer started to improve. He seemed more confident, and I thought we had turned a corner at last. When he brought friends home I'd hear laughter drifting down the hallway from his room and I'd breathe a sigh of relief. Things were going to be all right after all.

Then another milestone: David entered high school. The afternoon of his first day, I heard his footsteps along the walkway and I turned expectantly from the kitchen counter. David pushed open the door and dropped his backpack in the corner. He looked over at me and grinned, and I saw a sparkle in his eyes as he opened his mouth to speak. "Guess . . . guess what, Mom! I've join-joined the de-debate team."

His words made me stop cold and I shuddered as I listened to his faltering speech. It seemed like David had gone backward—his stammer had returned and now he wanted to speak in public! *He'll never make it,* I thought. *The pressure of competition will destroy him.*

"That's nice, dear," I said, hoping he couldn't see my hands tremble as I returned to washing vegetables in the sink. The very thing I'd tried to avoid over the years had finally caught up with me: David wanted to do his own thing regardless of the consequences. He was ready to grow up, explore new territory, and discover his strengths, even if it meant exposing his weaknesses. I knew he had to do it sometime, but was he ready now? Was I?

"I've got . . . got . . . to write a sp-speech before Sa-Saturday," he said, the stammer becoming more pronounced with every word. I stared out the kitchen window. How could he stand up and deliver a speech before a group of peers? How would he memorize it? He couldn't even remember a shopping list of four items let alone a prepared speech. I turned to face him, forcing a smile.

"How about if I help you get the speech off the ground," I said, trying to sound positive. "Then you can practice it and when you're ready I'll be your audience."

"Gee, th-thanks, Mom. You-you're the great-greatest."

For the next two days, David and I tossed ideas around and then he began writing the speech. By the following Wednesday he was ready to read his thoughts out loud. I listened and offered suggestions and then he returned to his computer to rework the paper. Once he was happy with it, he practiced and practiced. The night before the debate competition, I listened to his speech. After hearing it for two hours, I knew every word by heart.

The next morning, while David traveled with the team to the debate tournament some thirty miles away, I did everything to keep my mind off what he must've been going through. I baked cookies and brownies; I cleaned house and walked the dog. What if David let the team down, I obsessed. How would he cope with the teasing? I knew that the taunts from his peers at this age would be far more devastating than when he was a kid. Several hours later, I heard the front door open.

"Mom, are you home?" a familiar voice called. My heart pounded in my chest.

"How'd it go?" I called, wiping my hands on my apron and walking to the front room. The least I could do was show him how proud I was that he had participated. I stopped when I noticed the light from the open door shining on something silver in David's hands. "What's that?" I asked.

"It's my trophy, Mom." David held it up. "I took first place! And I didn't stammer once! The guys thought I did great . . . and you're great, too, Mom," he said, kissing me on the cheek. "If it weren't for all your help, I'd never have gotten through that speech!"

My heart soared. To see the sparkle in David's eyes and to hear his voice so full of confidence and joy was a miracle to me. As I wrapped my arms around my son and held him close, everything felt perfect—the day, the moment, and especially David. Everything I'd hoped for had come true for him. My little boy was becoming a man—a young man who had triumphed and come out a winner in every sense.

When Moms Are All Wet

Janet Konttinen

WHEN OUR SON JOINED the local swim team, he was one of the youngest members and took to the chilly temperatures and daily workouts like a duck to water. I asked what he liked best about swimming, and he said it was when his coach praised his efforts. What he liked least: the awkward silence that befell when he walked past his sisters wearing the required bikini-style Speedo swimsuit.

Months later, the whole team prepared to participate in a large out-of-town swim meet. Yes, I told him, there'd be lots of kids racing. Yes, there would be a snack stand.

When we arrived that Saturday morning the place was busy and friendly and my son immediately spied a dozen trophies on display. He asked if I thought he could win one. I took a closer look and found there was only one trophy for each age group of boys and another for girls. I didn't want him to feel defeated before he even started, but let's face it, him winning that trophy was about as likely as me medalling in Olympic bobsledding.

We checked in, and with all the events, heats, and lanes, it was a lot to keep track of. We learned that many of the older children used markers to note their schedules on the backs of their hands. My son also noticed that some of his teammates used the markers to write slogans across their arms or legs such as "Go Pirates" and "Eat My Bubbles." This regional swim meet was so much more exciting than those at our local pool. Here there were many experienced swimmers— not to mention real trophies, candy bars, and parents who let their kids write on themselves!

As the rest of our family found seats, my son got busy with his friends and the markers. The young boys tried to convey the old sports motto about "kicking butt" by writing the word "kick" across their backs with an arrow pointing down to their rumps. Unfortunately, many children read this message as "kick me here," and I saw my son get booted a dozen times. But he was in hog heaven and continued to scribble across the rest of his body until it was time for his first race. I held my breath as the gun sounded. In that instant, he looked so small and so completely ridiculous.

He swam his heart out, and when he finished, two officials handed him pieces of paper explaining he'd been disqualified for not touching the sides of the pool according to regulations. They were quick to point out that this was simply how a swim meet works. I wanted to point out how a sock in the mouth works.

Finally, on Sunday, it was time for the freestyle, his best stroke. He dove in beautifully and didn't take a breath until halfway down the pool. When his hand reached out and grabbed the other side, I looked up at the big scoreboard. He'd won the race! This time an official ran over and handed him an orange ribbon for winning the heat. My son was beaming, and I started crying.

I kept sobbing the whole time I dragged him outside the pool area over to the parking lot so I could, one, congratulate him, and two, get a grip on myself for God's sake. I could tell by the look on his face that I was definitely putting a damper on his victory bash with his buddies.

With my shoulders heaving, I tried to explain, "I'm sorry I'm crying honey, but I'm just so proud of you. Your daddy and I know you've worked very hard with your swimming. Did you know I swam every day when I was pregnant with you?"

"Yeah, you already told me that. Can we go back inside now?"

So what about the candy bars? That day he got two. The trophy? It's sitting on the shelf in his bedroom where I dust it off from time to time.

Karate Lessons

Lisa Mangini

MY HEART IS POUNDING. My palms are sweaty. It's my son's turn.

Slowly he approaches the judges. He bows respectfully. Then he launches a blizzard of kicks, lunges, punches, and movements that cause my eyes to blur and dance. It is Karate Tournament Day, and I am not doing so well.

My nine-year-old son has eagerly been awaiting this moment for six months. Every day he wakes and practices his moves. Every night before he goes to bed he runs through his combinations. Finally, he has found a sport about which he is passionate and something he does so well. And in a few moments of the judge's time, his motivation might be altered forever.

Hammerstrike, front kick, tiger claw. I am shaking.

He has been taught to do his best and to have fun. But it cannot be denied that today, this is a competition. He wins a point, but the match continues.

Side kick, dragon rake, back fist. The girl against whom he is sparring in this tournament wins a point. *Okay,* I think. *They're even.* My son responds with a series of kicks, strikes, and lunges. He throws her off guard. Point for my son. I breathe again.

The judges step in, and the match restarts. The girl moves an inch too close to my son's foot in his next kick. He gets a warning for contact. *Wait,* I want to scream. *She moved forward into his kick!* But I keep my silence.

I am discovering that although I can provide my son with many advantages in life, ultimately his success or failure will be the result of his own efforts. I am powerless. I cannot change the outcome of this match. All I can do is wait. And pray.

The match continues. Point for my son. He makes the semifinals and I physically feel myself relaxing. Joy and pride surge through me. He can do this! I go over to him, look into his jubilant face, and shake his hand. I give him the thumbs-up.

We wait for the next match. He is excited, happy, even ecstatic. I am a mess, but he is doing fine. He has tasted success at something he loves, and he eagerly anticipates more. I riffle through my purse for something to eat but come up empty. I watch the remaining matches. No one is as sharp or as focused or as fast as my son.

Finally, his name is called again. He spars against another girl, another purple belt, for the second match. He launches his assault aggressively. Immediate warning for contact.

I am on my feet, studying the judges, studying the moves. Side kick, dragon rake, back fist. The girl wins a point. Then my son. Then the girl. Then my son.

A man behind me says, "Wow, he is good." I take pride in that statement. Another person says something about this being a real match. It is a tough match. Both contestants are good, but I fervently hope my son will prevail.

Hammerstrike, front kick, back kick. Block. Lunge. Then it is over. Final point for the girl.

Slowly the realization hits me that my son might not have won. I check with my husband. No, he did not win, but our son does not realize yet that he will not come home with his long-awaited trophy. I stare at him in silent agony and think about what I will say to him. That it is all about sportsmanship. That in life we have good days and bad days. That you can't always win. That life just isn't fair sometimes.

Mostly I think about the blow this will be to my son. How can I choose the right words to cushion it and boost his confidence? Should I brush it off with a "win some, lose some" attitude? Or should I talk to him about the deep life lessons of today?

I look at him and am overcome by a huge surge of love. He is starting to realize that his name will not be called. It is dawning on him that he is not the best, not today.

I walk over to him. "You are a champion in my eyes," I say, feebly. I hold him and his tears start to flow. He now knows of his defeat.

"But Momma, I don't understand!" he says through his tears. "I did everything right." I don't understand either, but I know this is how life goes sometimes.

"Awesome match," one of the judges says. Someone else nods. I take my son in my arms and talk to him about how life isn't always fair. About how there is always a next time. About always doing your best.

"But Momma, I don't understand," he says again. "I *did* do my best."

"I know," I say weakly. "You were the best in my eyes."

He goes to get his medal for sportsmanlike participation, tears still welling up in his eyes. He wanted a trophy. *I* wanted that trophy for him—just to show him what he can accomplish in life when he sets his mind to it.

My husband takes our son, Michael-David, aside and focuses on what he has learned. He further explains that he never once in his life won a trophy. That gets a laugh. I tell him I never won anything until I was sixteen. That offers hope.

On the way out, I purchase several dollars' worth of patches, posters, and memorabilia to give him something to go home with. I'm not sure if he will retain any interest in any of these items, but I spend the money anyway. We walk out, disappointed but spirited.

As a consolation prize, we go to McDonald's. I let Michael-David eat his ice cream first because, after all, this was an upside-down day. We talk about what he learned at the tournament, about his medals for participation, about the experience of watching so many talented individuals perform their sport.

"But I still don't understand," offers my son, between spoonfuls.

I don't either. But I do know that life is about such seasoning experiences; that character is developed by setting goals and trying harder; that luck is a major ingredient in life's successes.

My son keeps his thoughts to himself on the drive home. My husband grabs a pizza; we watch a movie as a family, sitting all together on the sofa. Later that night, while looking over his consolation posters and patches, he says to me, "Thanks, Momma. You're the best."

My heart swells. "Thank you, Michael-David," I say with a smile.

"I did do my best, Momma. But next time I will do even better."

"That's right," I say affirmatively. "But you are already the best in my eyes."

"Goodnight, Mom," he says.

"Goodnight, champ," I say. He smiles a sleepy smile and I turn out the light. Tomorrow is another day.

I don't get any sleep, of course. But he does. He wakes up in the morning, and it is a brand-new day.

Michael-David is now ten years old and is a brown belt. He received a trophy at green belt level since this writing. His mom is learning to take all of this in stride and looks forward to his black belt accomplishment and many more karate tournaments in her future.

Teacher on the Mound

Linda Watts

I WATCH MY FIRST-BORN son, now grown and holding his beautiful new daughter—caring for her, playing with her, helping her take her first steps, and I wonder, *Where has my little boy gone? Is he still in there somewhere, or does he only exist in my memories?* As I watch, I rack my brain trying to remember some of life's lessons that might have made him the loving father he is today. Did I consciously teach and train him to be like this? Can I take any credit for who he is, or was it just the luck of the draw?

As a young boy, Jared was warm and caring—but when did he learn to show such concern for others? How did he develop such self-confidence—the ability to do his best in life without worrying too much about what others thought? As I try to think of how I might have influenced him as a child, my mind finally settles on a day many years ago when a great lesson was learned. Only, it was my son who was the teacher and I the student. It was the day Jared taught me that success isn't always about winning. And as I play the scene through my mind, it is clear that the qualities he exhibited then sustain him as a father today.

It was 1988 and a typically hot summer day in Northern California where my family lived. Jared, about age thirteen, was playing a Saturday afternoon baseball game. As chance would have it, during this particular game, his team had run out of eligible pitchers and the coach called Jared to go to the mound. My first motherly instinct was "Why him? He's not a pitcher!" But I guessed that the coach figured Jared was a strong athlete and could at least give the other team something to hit, even if he hadn't had much pitching experience. I was nervous for him, but I also had a lot of confidence in him—I knew he could dig down deep and pull something magical out of his pocket. I knew he had it in him to be a hero and win the game.

But this was not to be the game dreams are made of. Jared warmed up—at least he was throwing the ball across the plate for the catcher to catch. Pretty good for "not being a pitcher," I assured myself. Soon the game became a battle of sheer determination, which seemed to go on forever. Every pitch he threw ended up a ball instead of the strikes we were hoping for. After four balls, the batter walked to first base, and so it continued with every player who came up to bat.

I could tell Jared's arm was getting tired and sore, but the determination was still there as he threw ball after ball and watched the opposing players walk around the bases and cross home plate, adding to their growing score. I was squirming in my seat and started to worry about what the other parents were thinking. Perhaps because of my pride alone, I kept praying that the coach would pull Jared out.

Any mother knows how difficult it is to watch your child struggle at a task and fail. *Poor Jared*, I thought . . . *how humiliated he must feel . . . he'll never want to play again!* I ached for my son. And then suddenly it hit me: He was just a kid, and this was just a game—a game his team would lose. But it wasn't the end of the world.

When the game finally ended, I watched Jared walk into the dugout. Strangely, he looked like the same confident kid the coach had called to the mound a half-hour before. No earth-shattering experience for him, this was simply another day on the ball field, and he had done his best. No, he was no hero that day, but perhaps it was only the adults in his life that placed meaning on words like *hero*. To Jared, the only thing that mattered was that he'd been asked to do a job and he had quietly accepted the challenge.

Now, as I see him caring for his little family, I remember the importance of the lesson he taught that day. Success *isn't* always about winning; rather, it's about not quitting. It doesn't come about during monumental events in life but in simple moments of quiet courage, determination, and doing one's best. Success is about not giving up when things get tough, and it's about being devoted and committed to something you love. Baseball or family.

I'm grateful for the wisdom Jared passed on to me that day. Today—on or off the field—I am still his biggest fan.

Golden Rules

Bev Grasso

I LOOKED AT THE fistful of flowers in my young son's hand and my heart melted. He knew how to do that to me. But when I took them to put them in water, I saw that the blossoms still contained their root system, dangling oddly within clods of dirt. *Hmmm,* I thought to myself. *I wonder where these came from?* I had my answer soon enough when my neighbor informed me that my son had yanked the flowers from her newly planted yard. Apologies made. Replanting to do. Bruce was grounded for a week while I lectured him about respecting other's property.

It was very important to me as a parent to instill in my sons and daughter the value of respect—respect for other people's feelings, their belongings, their privacy—basically, to abide by the simple rule of "do unto others." Honesty, thoughtfulness, and kindness were simple enough principles to grasp even at a young age, I believed. But clearly, my son Bruce was not getting it.

While relaxing in front of the TV one night, I heard a knock at my door. Several people from our apartment building had come to tell me their power had gone out. "That's odd," I said. "Mine's working fine." When it happened a second night, there were more knocks on the door and more than a few raised eyebrows. My other son, Brian, finally confessed—he had gone to the circuit breakers and flipped everyone's electricity off except ours, which was "too high to reach." More angry neighbors. More apologies. More grounding.

After a while, Bruce and Brian seemed to be doing better and I was breathing easier again. Maybe all was not lost and there was hope that they were internalizing some of what I was desperately trying to teach. So as a reward, I sent Bruce off one morning to the corner grocery store to buy some crayons. Soon he was back home with a packet of art supplies far more expensive than the change he'd taken with him. Not only that, but when I checked his pockets, I found the money I'd given him stuffed deep down inside. Back to the store we went to return the merchandise and apologize to the manager. On the way home, though, I decided to make one more stop.

Call it a desperate move. Call it overboard. All I knew was that my two sons needed to learn a lesson once and for all. I made a quick stop at the local police station and asked the friendly officer if he could lock my sons up for a short time. I wanted them to get a glimpse of real criminal life and experience for a few minutes what was ahead of them if their pranks persisted.

Did Bruce ever steal again? No, never. Did Brian learn respect for other's property? Yes, finally he did. Today they are both model citizens in spite of their rough start. Although I wouldn't trade a single moment with any of my children, raising my daughter was like riding on a merry-go-round compared to the roller-coaster ride of raising my sons—exciting *and* scary! But with a mother's watchful eye, a little creative discipline, and a lot of prayer, Bruce and Brian have grown up to make their mother proud. In fact, just the other day one of them brought me a lovely bouquet of flowers. Neatly trimmed, no roots—I did a quick check just to be sure. The neighbor's garden looked just fine.

Baby Mine

Lynne Marie Rominger

IN THE DISNEY CLASSIC *Dumbo*, the mother pachyderm waits patiently for her baby boy to finally arrive. She opens the blanket, and, there before her, sits her little one. Huge eyes, sweet smile, and precocious personality—Dumbo is perfect to his mother, Mrs. Jumbo, even if ridiculed by the other elephants, animals, and humans for his "defect" of exceptionally large and funny-looking ears. He's "different," after all. Although his difference seems like an insurmountable obstacle for Dumbo and Mommy, in the end, the little elephant's ears emerge as his strength. Indeed, early on, when all those others didn't see the beauty in her baby boy, Mrs. Jumbo somehow stepped back to appreciate him as beautiful and worthy. I wish I had been more like her when my own firstborn, Nickolaus, arrived.

When I brought Nickolaus home from the hospital, I

admit that I felt something was amiss—something was unique about my little guy. Certainly, I was proud! In my arms, curled next to me, cuddling in to my chest, seemed the perfect child by all societal standards—perfect Apgar score, perfect coloring, perfect cry, perfect number of fingers and toes. Indeed, even during my pregnancy, I remember harboring self-righteous sentiments that this child was meant to do something great. Little did I realize how correct my intuition was—except that the greatness Nickolaus is currently developing is of a slightly different nature than I had envisioned.

My son suffers from Pervasive Developmental Disorder, Not Otherwise Specified (PDD-NOS), a neurodevelopmental disorder currently on the autism spectrum. His difficulties run the gamut from violent outbreaks to an inability to pick up on normal social cues and conversations. He remains a challenge for me every day, and it has only been within the last few months that I've recognized how my selfishness has thwarted his growth and prevented me from seeing the incredible love and sensitivity my "difficult" child was attempting to share with me.

Initially, I had no reason to believe something was afoot. The differences my child exhibited could be seen as within normal parameters. Babies are often fussy, demanding, throw tantrums, are picky eaters, tend to scream and cry when things don't go their way, and generally drive their mothers mad, right? When Nickolaus refused to take Christmas pictures one year, I rationalized that he was entering the terrible twos. Though his diet consisted of little more than cucumber pieces and cheese pizza, I offered to nosy relatives that I, too, was picky eater as a child. Moreover, he seemed to play normally; he held an intense fascination with trains. He loved trains so much that daily he insisted we watch *Dumbo* just for the scenes with "Casey Jr. comin' down the track, comin' down the track, with a smoky stack!"

But I couldn't explain his extreme behavior when he was around other children. In a toy store as he played with a Brio train set, another toddler approached the display. Nickolaus immediately clutched at my legs shyly, then fell to the ground screeching. His grandparents and I left the store perplexed, and the fit—that turned into rage—lasted more than an hour. But I refused to admit anything was wrong with Nickolaus. I wrapped all my fears away and noted the exceptional aspects of my son as leverage that he didn't need help.

Unfortunately, when kindergarten arrived, so did the frequency of outbursts. His tentative nature in social situations caused him to cope in the classroom in numerous ways; Nick proved the funny guy, the disruptive guy, and the volatile guy. After my first I.E.P. (Individual Education Plan), where my son's behaviors were outlined by a panel of teachers as "manipulative," I began to research and seek help for him; I knew in my heart he wasn't manipulative. I also couldn't believe that my child—who refused to watch Pokémon because the characters terrified him—was now threatening to harm other children.

My gut knew that Nickolaus was suffering and lashing out because of his shyness and lack of social skills, but I began to worry that he was being picked on because of his unusual personality. One day, I arrived early and watched as the whole class participated in an athletic skills test. In horror, I heard the teacher call out Nick's name and berate him in front of all the other kids for "being bad"! I knew my son, as any child with special needs, created extra work for the teacher, but it seemed that she was taking her frustrations out on him. Consequently, Nickolaus began loathing school and feeling ostracized. After three years, four different schools, and several psychologists' evaluations, he was finally placed in a "cocooned" classroom environment, a Special Day Class, where his needs are somewhat met.

Though I always advocated for Nickolaus in an educational setting, my patience at home was lacking. For years, I resented the extra time needed to attend psych appointments, I.E.P. meetings, and just to deal with Nickolaus's idiosyncrasies. One morning might find me begging him to attend school, while in the afternoon he wreaked combat on his younger sisters for doing something as innocuous as pointing at him. Forget about doctor appointments and medical treatment! Until recently, each illness rivaled the Battle of Gettysburg. His refusal to take amoxicillian for an ear infection resulted in an emergency room visit where doctors held him down and injected Nick with ample doses of the prescription. Each day was emotionally exhausting, and eventually, I found myself shutting down to him, finding ways to spend less time with him and pitying myself, instead of trying to understand my child whose brain functioned like a Mac in a PC world. That was my reaction until recently.

A few months ago, I took my whole family to the Disney Store with the promise that each child could pick out one item. My three-year-old twins, Faith and Hope, rushed the premises, grabbing everything and asking for anything within their reach. My six-year-old, Sophia, targeted the princess collection and passionately pleaded for several ensembles. Nickolaus, now eight, looked contemplatively around and chose nothing. Finally, his eyes caught sight of a stuffed animal. No Buzz Lightyear or medieval weaponry for him, but instead a soft, blue-eyed elephant with oversize ears. Quietly, he asked, "Can I have this? Is it okay, Mommy?"

Suddenly, I realized how sweet this child really was—at his core. I began thinking about his wonderful and sensitive attributes. He has never played "war." He has never watched a violent cartoon in his life. There are no X-Box rants from his lips. He still believes in Santa Claus wholeheartedly, along with the tooth fairy. He prefers letting the wind blow on his face on a swing to a competitive team sport. Each night, Nickolaus is the child who still nuzzles up to me and refuses to allow societal pressure to force him out of Mommy's hugs and kisses in public.

So at the moment Nickolaus clutched his Dumbo purchase, I realized how his strengths had existed right in front of me for eight years and I had failed to see them. Suddenly, it became tremendously important for me to talk to Nickolaus, to spend time with him, to read to him, to sit with him, and to love him. My eyes have finally opened. I am blessed, not forsaken, with a child who possesses PDD-NOS, for he has taught me patience, acceptance, and unconditional love. His innocence remains while other grade-schoolers run the track to sophistication and worldliness at a dizzyingly, unfortunate pace.

Dumbo now sits on Nick's dresser next to his bed. At night, when Nickolaus is asleep, I often crawl into bed next to him, wrap him in my arms, and sing, *"If they knew sweet*

*little you, they'd end up loving you, too; And those same peo-
ple who scold you, what they'd give for just the right to hold
you, baby mine."*

I wish I'd sung it sooner.

PART SIX

Ties That Bind

"Parents are like shuttles on a loom. They join the threads of the past with threads of the future and leave their own bright patterns as they go."

—Fred Rogers

Exchange of Gifts

Elaine Reiser Alder

"IT'S TIME TO GO now, Mom," he called through the front door. "Better get some gloves on, 'cause it's getting kind of cold out here."

The mid-winter gray and the streetlights defied the time. It was just five o'clock, and my son, the pint-size newspaper carrier, had been folding and putting rubber bands on his ninety papers since he came home from school. Now he packed them sardine-tight into a double bag; the single bag was for me.

He called from the porch again, "Let's get going before it's dark."

For Christmas, we gave "gifts of self" that year. When I asked eleven-year-old Nate what would be most special for me to give him, he didn't hesitate. "Come with me on my paper route, will you?" His impish grin forewarned that it would be memorable.

Ironically, I scheduled the day to give my gift without knowing it would follow the season's biggest snowstorm. So, with dinner simmering in the oven and our bodies bundled against the cold, we headed down the street. Twenty inches of snow lay on the ground, a slight breeze wisping its surface into featherlike drifts. It was two blocks to the first door, then a ramble through the student trailer court, breaking trails in the fresh snow.

Drifting snowflakes added a holiday atmosphere to the dusk, while little Christmas lights in trailer windows told us that mini-families on shoestring incomes lived inside. Their gift-giving, like their monthly newspaper bill, would be carefully budgeted, and their Christmas trees and window decorations signaled traditions handed on to a new generation.

My bag was heavy, though my seventy-pound guide bore the double burden. His year's experience as a carrier had taught him all the tricks, including how to tote a bag with papers balanced front and back. He suggested that I deliver on one side of the road as he called out the numbers to me. He would do the opposite side.

The first few trailers were fun. There is a simple satisfaction to a paper route—service, orderliness, completion.

"See that trailer?" my sidekick asked as he pointed toward the small, metal home. "They had a baby this week."

"How do you know?"

"Well, when I collected from them I could tell she was going to. Then they printed it in the window with shoe polish," he reported.

As an afterthought, he said, "It was a girl."

A few steps more and he remarked, "I don't like to collect from the people in this trailer."

"Why?" I puzzled.

"Oh, . . . they don't seem to have very much money."

"What makes you think that?"

"They always get it out of a fruit bottle. Sometimes it's all in pennies and dimes."

We walked along in silence for a few moments.

"I just wish I didn't have to collect from people who don't have much money. It kind of makes me feel sad." I was moved by his sensitivity.

As the snow fell thicker and the bags became lighter, the calves of my legs felt tight and my boots irritated the skin. The novelty was beginning to wear off, the trailer court looked much bigger. But I had to admit that the snow was postcard pretty and the company charming.

"These people are really neat," he began as he placed a paper on one porch.

"How come?"

"Whenever I collect from them they give me a cupcake or a cookie. They always make me feel like I'm important," he added self-consciously.

We trudged along without a word for many minutes. But my mind was anything but blank: *He gets three cents per paper per night for this . . . No wonder he hates to get up at six on Sunday mornings . . . If only his customers knew what a sacrifice this is . . . Is it really worth all this effort every day?*

My musings were interrupted when Nate asked, "Mom, what is frankincense and myrrh?"

Surprised, I tried to answer. "What does that have to do with a paper route?" I teased.

"Nothing. But we were talking about it in Sunday School. They're sure different-sounding words, aren't they?"

So we talked about frankincense and myrrh. That was good for a few more trailers.

"Do you know who lives there?" He pointed to a trailer.

"No," I replied. To me these were all just numbers on an emergency list tacked to the bulletin board at home.

"The USU quarterback. I'll bet he makes All-American next year; he's so good. He used to be one of my customers, but then he stopped. I don't know why. I sure wish he still was." He grinned. "I told all my friends at school that I was his paperboy. They thought that was pretty cool."

I was dragging along, but he ran ahead to a cluster of out-of-the-way trailers.

"Just a minute, Mom," he called. "I've got to put these in the milk boxes. These customers don't like their papers left on the porch." *Now what? They even expect extra service?* A little farther on, he showed me a trailer where "Dad's secretary lives" and another where "she saves the rubber bands for me." Two trailers beyond he said, "These people gave me a Christmas card and a plate of cookies last week."

Around the corner he showed me where "one of Dad's students lives. He asked me if we were related when he wrote my name on the check."

He stopped at the next trailer. "Something sad happened to this family," he said as he walked toward the door.

"What was that?"

"Do you remember when I told you about the little baby who died? This is where that family lives."

"Yes, and I remember cutting out the obituary from the paper. Did you take it to them?"

"I did. But it was sort of hard to know what to say to them. He was the only baby they had."

We neared the end of the route, but he had one more hero to tell me about.

"Did I tell you that I've got a golf champion on my route? He won the tournament. Look in that living room window. See all those trophies? He's just in college, but he'll probably be a pro."

"What's he like?"

"He's nice. His wife is always telling me she appreciates it when I get the paper right by the door. They've got a cute little girl, too. They aren't hard to talk to, even though he's important."

By now, we were ready to leave the trailer court. It was nice having a lighter bag on my shoulder, and I was sure Nate felt better with his bag nearly empty, too.

"Well, that's the trailer court. I'll show you an easy way to the dorms, where I have a few more customers." Tromping through an adjoining field, we looked like two white ragamuffins.

"Let's make tracks though here," Nate called as he moved ahead of me. "There's nothing in the snow. I'll go first. I love to do this between the trailers on a snowing day," he informed me.

We trudged, single file; I aimed for his footprints. Then he turned around toward me.

"It's more fun to deliver in the new snow than anything."

"What?" I wasn't sure I had heard him correctly.

"Oh, you know. Making tracks and watching snow fall by the streetlights. It's kind of warm and soft and quiet."

I felt silly for feeling the cold instead of appreciating the setting.

In a moment of awe, I began to genuinely appreciate this little boy with his computer memory, knowing exactly which dorms to stop at when they looked like a sea of identical buildings to me. *I hope he never gets sick,* I thought. *There's no way we'd be able to substitute for him and come out even on the papers.*

"Well, we're done," he said as he delivered the last paper. "Wasn't too bad, was it?" he asked, sensing my amazement that we hadn't run short or quit along the way.

"Pretty neat customers, aren't they?"

"Sure are," I agreed.

"And you give nice Christmas presents, Mom," he confided. "It's more fun when there's someone to talk to."

The gifts were manifold that day. My gift was time and company; his was a message that years of mothering had not been wasted; his customers have him trust in humanity and confidence in himself.

"Next Christmas will you give me two days, Mom?"

"Why not?" I squeezed his gloved hand extra tight, warming inside with pride, even renewal.

Sometimes the best gifts aren't wrapped in paper and bows. And sometimes the giver gains the most.

Stuffed Angel

Rosemary Roberts

YOU COULD SEE IT in his grin or in the pause of a deep thought . . . he was his grandfather's boy. Almost as if they had rehearsed it before he was born, my son, Sean, bore a striking resemblance to my father in his demeanor and expression—that of a southern gentleman with Tennessee charm and simple elegance, cleft chin and all.

Their bond had been an instant one since diapers, something I became increasingly grateful for as years passed. I was a single, divorced mother, and my father was Sean's primary male role model. Every social or ethical dilemma found Sean asking himself the repeated question, "What would Papa do?" Following in his grandfather's footsteps, he stood courageous against bigger, older, would-be bullies—even when outnumbered three to one. He lived to make Papa proud, and proud he was.

Sean also marveled at the wisdom of his first-grade teacher. He was especially in awe of her ability to turn a book around displaying the picture on the page to the class and reciting at the same time the words on that page without looking. He was so amazed by this feat that he decided to practice the art himself.

Up in his room, Sean's audience consisted of his stuffed animals, of which there were many. He lined up all his bears, in the order of their social hierarchy, of course, with the smaller ones sitting up front. And he decided to critique his presence of speech and dramatic ability as well, recording his readings and then reviewing them afterward.

Now Papa, more likely to shower Sean with stocks and bonds or fishing gear than with gifts of toys, was impressed with his reading efforts and while shopping one day noticed an unusual-looking stuffed bear. The toy animal sported a nice tie and round-rimmed glasses—an intellectual bear, indeed. So Papa bought the bear and brought him home to Sean. "He looks older than the rest," Sean declared, and decided to call him George. From that point on, George took a prominent place among the other bears during Sean's readings.

Six months had passed, and Papa, having recently been diagnosed with a respiratory condition, called one night to say he wasn't feeling well; that he was going to rest and would I call in an hour to check on him. Waiting for the hour to pass was dreadful, but when it finally arrived, I began calling . . . no answer. I tried again, and still he did not answer.

Fearful that I shouldn't have waited, that he might be in need of help, I called a neighbor to come stay with Sean so I could drive the short distance to Papa's house.

It was a stormy night with rain blowing sideways in the wind. Sean was angry that I wouldn't let him go with me. "He's my Papa!" he cried. But I was afraid of what I might find and thought it better if Sean stayed behind.

As I backed out of my gravel driveway, my headlights lit up Sean's small, barefoot figure running out into the rain, George the Bear in tow. Stopping, I rolled down my window and yelled at him to get back inside, but still his little feet kept coming. When he reached the car, he handed me George through the window, and as his tears mixed with raindrops he said, "Take George to Papa. If he has to go to the hospital he won't be alone."

That was fifteen years ago, and from that day forward George was never far from my father's side. He rode shotgun in Dad's motor home during summer-long fishing adventures and spent many nights in the hospital with him, too. When Dad's bed was made, he would place George on top with his legs crossed, for character I guess. My first inkling of Dad's emotional bond with this bear came when he was sick with the flu and fighting a relentless fever. I mentioned George, who was momentarily sitting on Dad's headboard. "George," he said, as if speaking about a dear friend. "Good ol' George always takes good care of me." With that he placed George under the covers and tucked him in.

The bond between Sean and my father continued to be something of great importance to them both, and the bear that had once been a gift from a grandfather to his grandson was more important to my father than either Sean or I could have ever imagined.

Dad died last year of a brain tumor, a sudden and devastating blow to Sean. In his final weeks, it was necessary to keep George the Bear where Dad could see him at all times. As the end neared, speech had become almost impossible for Dad. Sometimes the words were there but he couldn't speak them. Sometimes the words just disappeared mid-stride. But the day before he passed away, Dad experienced a moment of clarity in which he declined further medication and then spoke to Sean privately; a rare moment he said that many grandfathers don't get as they prepare to depart. He told Sean what it had meant to have him in his life, how proud he was of him, and what great things he thought he was capable of in his life ahead.

Afterward, he had me position his right arm, now limp and numb to all sensation, in a certain position. "Perfect," he said softly. Then he had me tuck George under the covers beside him and promise that under no circumstances would anyone move him until he was gone. I promised.

The next afternoon, I brushed my father's hair from his forehead and told him that now would be a good time to take a walk with me and George; that we'd go as far with him as we could, but that he was to just keep on going and know that George would take care of us in his absence and that everything would be okay. With that, he was at peace and he left us.

It is, they say, the simple acts of love that sustain us, and some of the purest are those between a grandfather and his grandson. Sean, now twenty-one years old, still bears the image of his grandfather's grin or his pause in the midst of deep thought. And George, well, he's on the bed just as my dad preferred him, with one leg crossed over the other.

Lucky Number 13

Julie Larson

THERE WERE ONLY two people in the world who could break through the tough exterior of my oldest son, Taylor: his baby sister and his Grandma Gaye. Taylor had a special repoire with his grandma ever since he was a little baby, and as his quiet, serious nature developed during his childhood, Grandma Gaye was the one who could soften him up and joke around with him better than anyone else. Taylor was her thirteenth grandchild, and she dubbed him "Lucky Number 13," so he saw himself as being pretty special in her eyes.

A typical boy, Taylor always loved sports—all kinds of sports, but especially basketball. Since the time he played nonstop with his Fisher-Price beginner's hoop, he almost worshipped anything and everything to do with the game. Because we lived in Arizona, we were all Phoenix Suns fans—

especially Grandma Gaye. And Taylor and Grandma talked basketball every chance they got.

Although Gaye suffered from rheumatoid arthritis and only had one lung, which was frequently infected, she was an avid fan at Taylor's basketball games as he grew up. Year after year her health deteriorated, but she'd make it to as many of his games as possible, cheering along with the rest of us from the bleachers. She often remarked that her one wish was to live long enough to see Taylor play on the high school team.

Just before Taylor's thirteenth birthday, however, Grandma Gaye's heart finally gave out. She died peacefully during the night, but I decided not to tell my boys until after school the next afternoon. I was especially nervous about telling Taylor, so I took him aside and tried to tell him as gently as I could. He showed no emotion at all—he was stone cold, as if the news hadn't even registered. He didn't want to talk about it; he didn't want to hear about her; he just went about his usual routine as if nothing unusual had happened. His demeanor didn't change for the next several days—all the way until the funeral. I kept wondering and worrying about when it was going to hit him and how he'd handle it after keeping it pent up for so long.

As we filed into the church the day of the funeral, we sat down as a family in one of the front pews and my eyes kept wandering over to check on Taylor. As soon as he was seated, his head dropped and the dam broke. He sobbed noticeably and uncontrollably, and no one seemed to know how to help him. Although I knew this was what he needed, I ached for him and wished I had a way to magically ease his pain. As the service progressed, he eventually got control, and by the end of the funeral, seemed to have retreated into his cold, hard shell that protected him from any feelings.

Then Saturday came—basketball game day. I was still worried about Taylor and how he was dealing with his grief. Twelve was such a confusing, emotional age. He was too old to cuddle and comfort, distract with fun activities or ice-cream cones, but too young to understand that in time, he would heal.

He walked out of his room that morning all suited up for his YMCA game—ready to go except for his shoes. Those he held in his hand along with a black marking pen. I watched him set the shoes on the kitchen counter and write "#13" on the edge of one sole. On the other edge where everyone could see it, he carefully penned "G.G."

No words were said about the message on his shoes, but Taylor played the game of his life that day. In my heart, I knew Grandma Gaye was there to watch every move he made on the court. More important, I felt certain that Taylor knew his grandma was there to receive her special tribute from a loving grandson, who would miss her for a long, long time.

The Overcoat

Sara Camilli

L OVE BETWEEN PARENTS and their offspring is not a tangible thing, but is rather expressed in the everyday things that parents—and grandparents—do for their children like fixing meals, listening to their hopes and fears, and attending ball games. However, a tangible item can come to represent love as it evokes a memory of the person to whom it belonged or who gave it away.

Such has been the case with Grandpa's overcoats. To his grandsons, they have become a symbol of Grandpa himself.

Our boys grew up about ten minutes away from their grandparents, who gladly baby-sat on many occasions, forging a strong bond between the generations. And what our boys learned from their grandparents could not have been taught as well by anyone else—lessons not consciously taught, but taught by example; lessons of patience, thrift, and, most important, respect. Our boys respected their grandparents because their grandparents respected them, glorying in each accomplishment and celebrating their uniqueness.

They learned about the cycles of life by helping Grandma and Grandpa in their huge garden and delighted in sharing the harvest they had helped produce. Though we might have discarded something worn or broken, our sons learned at their grandparents' house that those things might have a future life. Grandpa fixed what was broken while Grandma mended what was torn. Nothing was wasted. Our three boys observed the liners of cereal boxes and bread wrappers being cleaned out and used for sandwiches or cookies when a picnic lunch was packed. When a packing box was needed, Grandpa knew just where to find one of the right size. On a sunny day, the boys helped hang clothes on the line even though Grandma had a dryer. The best Christmas gift my husband ever received was a recycled one from his parents—a shoe box full of boyhood treasures found in the attic— a treasured gift of memories.

So it should have been no surprise that when one of our sons grew up and had his first job, Grandpa went into one of the closets and pulled out a wool overcoat from the 1940s, still in perfect condition, and said to our son, "You'll be needing something more professional-looking than your ski jacket. This will keep you nice and warm." I think all the boys were a bit skeptical that this coat would actually ever be worn. It was, after all, from so long ago. But our son, out of great respect, graciously accepted the gift and hung it in his closet. And lo and behold, on a bitterly cold day, when he knew a suit wouldn't possibly keep him warm, our son put it on. He was astonished to find that others loved the coat. He got many compliments on it and found that people were even more attracted to it once they learned it had belonged to his grandfather. The coat had become a badge of honor.

Now another son was starting a job in cold New England. He had borrowed the coat on occasion and was sad that he, too, didn't have one. When I mentioned this fact to Grandpa, he said, "You know, I think for some reason I had two of those coats." He searched the closets, and sure enough, there was another coat very similar to the first.

Through the years, those coats have served the boys well, and they now delight in telling Grandpa where his coats have gone—to Holland, Japan, Argentina, and Hong Kong. Wherever they travel, the boys are wrapped in Grandpa's love and feel the warmth of his admiration and respect for them.

We have three sons, and, unfortunately, Grandpa only had two coats. However, the third son became a swing dancer, and for him, Grandpa found a hat from 1946, still in its box with the sales ticket. It cost a princely sum back then—$15.46. He must've bought it for a very special occasion. When our son was photographed for the newspaper wearing the hat in a dance demonstration, there was one person who had to get a copy of the article—Grandpa, of course. His reply when he saw it was, "I guess I'll have to up the rent on the hat now that it's bringing you such notoriety!"

Though the boys only see Grandpa now about twice a year instead of two or three times a week, they have only to hold in their hands the things that were Grandpa's to bring back a flood of happy memories. In their eyes, those articles of clothing have increased in value through the years—mostly in the value of the lessons taught by a devoted grandfather.

Inseparable

Julie Elsberry

L IFE WAS RELATIVELY simple after my first son was born. Our little band of three had the normal health challenges and financial worries of most young families, but it wasn't until sons number two and number three came along eighteen months apart that I knew the real meaning of the word *challenge*. Because my husband worked odd hours, I was left at home with no car and three young boys to feed, bathe, and tuck in every night alone. By the end of each day, I felt I hadn't accomplished much more than sitting in the same chair all day, rocking or comforting or cuddling one or the other of the youngest boys. I remember changing the words to an old childhood song and I'd sing it over and over as I rocked them, feeling much sorrier for myself than the words indicated.

I have two little boys in my one little lap,
My life would be simpler if they'd just take a nap.
If Trevor were happy and Jacob were, too,
Then one grateful mom would have nothing to do!

I recall one day in particular when my three little boys and I were, of necessity, in the bathroom together. Trevor, two, was in the bathtub, and because I couldn't leave him unattended, I sat on the toilet, breast-feeding hungry baby Jacob while going over homework with Taylor, six, who sat on the floor next to me. Not exactly a setting for a Norman Rockwell painting. Suddenly, Trevor's face turned the shade of red that warned of an imminent "potty" accident, so I quickly broke the suction Jacob had on me, passed him over to Taylor, and tried to get Trevor on the toilet in time. Too late. So much for trying to dovetail my motherly duties.

I quickly decided that in order to survive my family circumstances with a shred of sanity, I'd need to get the two youngest boys on the same schedule. Soon, they were eating together, napping together, bathing together, and going to bed promptly at 7 P.M. together. This led to a great bond between them—they were a matched set. Trevor never went to a friend's house unless Jacob could come along. When Jacob was old enough to walk, Trevor took him on a tour of the backyard. Holding his little hand, Trevor proudly delivered the whole spiel: "Over there is the swing set, and this is Mommy's garden, and that tree is the one that's fun to play under, and those rocks are sharp when you don't have shoes on," and so on. They were buddies in every sense.

Somewhere along the line, however, it dawned on Trevor

that because he was two years older, he should have more privileges than Jacob, and that he should naturally be better at everything simply by virtue of his age. This started a competition between my two boys that was, at times, beneficial (who could read more books, do mental-math the quickest, etc.) but more often, unbearable (who could stay up the latest, collect the most baseball cards, etc.). At first it seemed like it might pay off: If one of the boys needed to improve his grades or his scouting, reading, or piano lessons, all it took was for his brother to start working at it and the race was on! Unfortunately, the competition would get out of hand and a barrage of arguing and name-calling would ensue.

The constant bickering and teasing were driving me crazy until one day, in a flash of inspiration, I remembered what my mother-in-law had done with my husband and his brother when they used to argue as boys. It seemed unlikely that it would solve my problem, but I was at my wit's end and ready to try anything.

The next time Trevor and Jacob had a particularly bad day when nothing seemed to help them be friendly, I told them they needed to sit on the couch for fifteen minutes and I would set the timer. The condition was, though, that they had to sit with their arms around each other for the entire time.

"What?" Trevor shrieked, "you want me to put my arms around that little creep?" Total disgust filled both of their faces, but Jacob made the first move with a very tentative hug. When Trevor finally realized that the timer wouldn't start until his arms were around his brother, he acquiesced. Awkward at first, it wasn't long before the two boys were giggling and joking as they lived out their "sentence." Afterward, they were best of buddies for the rest of the day.

Since that day, it has never failed. The "hugging time-out" worked every time, and the need for it has decreased dramatically. Most of the time they're inseparable—looking out for each other at school, helping each other with projects, playing and laughing together like the best of friends. Having three sons so close together was a challenge, indeed, but with some creativity here and there—and a little help from a wise mother-in-law—I've decided I wouldn't have it any other way.

Rites of Passage

Denise Roy

ON THIS OTHERWISE ordinary night at the end of July, the men in my life are out under the stars beating drums in a redwood forest.

Okay, actually, I'm the one with the drum. But I thought drumming sounded more dramatic than "the men in my life are out under the stars eating steaks in a redwood forest."

Yesterday, my husband, his best friend, my two brothers-in-law, and five teenage boys packed up the minivans and headed out for what is now the annual Men's Weekend. This tradition began six years ago when our oldest son, Ben, turned thirteen. Puberty was turning Ben inside out, stretching him, changing his voice and his biceps, morphing him into an adult before our eyes. We wanted to find some way to mark this transition, to celebrate this rite of passage.

Some men never hear their father's stories or receive their father's blessing. They do not hear their elders say: *"We see you. Your life is important. What you say should be heard."* Perhaps I am overly sensitized to this. As a therapist, I hear over and over about what life is like for people who've never been acknowledged by their parents as a mature adult. They walk around with an empty space inside, usually looking in all the wrong places for the message that they are good and whole and blessed.

There is no ready-made formula for giving such a blessing. Life in our American melting pot often lacks meaningful rituals. Most of our ancestors' wisdom has been boiled away, replaced with bland consumerism. But by borrowing from one tradition and taking from another, we were able to piece together a ritual to affirm Ben's spiritual and emotional passage into manhood.

The older men took Ben camping in a redwood forest. They went on hikes, built fires, and talked into the night. My husband, who had been reading a number of books about men's psychology, wrote out a list of questions intended to spark conversation on what it means to be a man:

> *Who are my heroes?*
> *What gives meaning to my life?*
> *What qualities do I value in a relationship?*
> *What are my dreams for myself?*
> *What is my idea of power?*
> *What is the source of my power?*
> *What are my gifts?*
> *What do I fear?*

What is sacred?
What does success mean to me?
What brings me joy?
For what, or whom, would I sacrifice my time,
my energy, my health, my life?

I heard that the sharing was richer and deeper than any had imagined it would be. My son looked older when he returned; he looked as if he had a new self-respect and new understanding. That first weekend was six years ago, and since then, three other boys have reached the age of thirteen, and now each of them attends subsequent weekends as one of the men. On this July night, the fifth boy is receiving the blessing from his elders. He is being seen for who he is and is getting the message that who he is matters. He is listening to stories about what it means to be a man and is beginning to understand that his story is part of a larger story. In the telling of the tales, he is becoming part of a legacy.

I don't think it's an accident that all this is happening under redwood trees. We are fortunate to live near the California coast, where redwoods have grown for twenty million years. These trees have trunks that are incredibly strong and resistant to fire, insects, and disease. They often grow close together, their roots intertwined like fingers, providing them stability despite their great height. I imagine that bits of redwood bark and needles fall down upon this little group of men, getting in hair and tents and shoes. Perhaps these giants of the forest are imparting some part of their great strength, adding depth and breadth and height to those human beings who've come to visit.

All I know is that when the men return, it will seem as if they've internalized the forest. Smelling of smoke and perspiration, my teenage men will wrap their long, branchy arms around my shoulders and say, "It was good." When I ask for more details, they'll just smile, give a little squeeze, and repeat in a deep and rooted voice, "It was good."

They'll have been gone just forty-eight hours, and I'll try to piece together some of what those hours held. I'll develop the roll of film at the drugstore, then scour the pictures for information. If it's anything like last year, I'll see a photo of eight males walking with their shirts tied around their heads and their shorts pulled down extra low, the older men showing their underwear in solidarity with the teens. I'll hear stories of daylong hikes, of Ranger Bob coming four times to quiet the camp, of campfire breakfasts of bacon and fresh coffee. I'll hear that the young men were eloquent as they spoke of love and life and God. I'll see sunburned noses and dirty vans. I'll smell smoke on their jackets and sleeping bags, and I'll refuse to do the laundry. Eventually, I'll change my mind, then I'll smile when I find bits of redwood clinging to their clothes.

I am filled with a deep peace, grateful that my sons have interconnected roots with their older men. My sons know that they'll never be alone; they know that they have men in their lives with whom they can share struggles and joys. I witness this connection in the long, deep hugs and pats on the back they give one another as they leave to go home.

Like the redwoods, these young men will grow straight and tall. They will take in the blessing of this weekend, they will blossom, and, in turn, they will bless the world. They already tell me that they will do this ritual for their sons.

I, too, am blessed.

I am the mother of men.

PART SEVEN

The Journey

"Every boy has an inner timetable for growth—a pattern unique to him ... Growth is not steady, forward, upward progression. It is instead a switchback trail; three steps forward, two back, one around the bushes, and a few simply standing, before another forward leap."

—Dorothy Corkville Briggs

My Superman

Linda Dobson

AS THE ELDEST of my three homeschooled children, Chuck spent years with me clearing the way through uncharted learning territory, ever on the lookout for educational projects from which he could glean significant knowledge as he rapidly grew from baby to child to adolescent. Certainly we jumped at anything that bolstered academic instruction, but equally important were activities that put him out and about in our friendly community and provided opportunities to work with adults to hone the skills that would prepare him for his own adulthood.

One of Chuck's Boy Scout troop leaders was also a volunteer fireman who arranged for Scouts to study and train alongside the "real" volunteers. At age fourteen, Chuck was just old enough to sign on, and we agreed participation would be an educational, as well as exciting, experience.

Little did I know what we were getting into. Don't ever let the word *volunteer* fool you; between meetings, training exercises, classes for both firefighters and emergency medical technicians, actual fire and rescue calls, and events to help raise the funds to keep the department functioning, Chuck (and I, as honorary chauffeur) put in more hours each month than many part-time jobs require. Mind you, Chuck didn't have to be at everything, but neither wild horses nor my car broken down on the road in the middle of the night on the way to a fire would stop him. (A fellow firefighter taking the same route to the firehouse gave Chuck a lift. I, on the other hand, was left to walk home—in my pajamas.)

Time flew, but after three years of his devoted attention to firefighting and rescue work, I could look at my son leaning into the refrigerator in his Mets baseball cap and still see a little boy running around the backyard in his Superman Underoos shirt with a receiving blanket cape around his neck for good measure. With the help of officer friends in the department, Chuck discovered that although the by-laws unmistakably stated one needed to be eighteen years old to be a member, a less frequently used section declared that, if parental permission was provided, the department members could vote to allow a seventeen-year-old to join. Until now, even though Chuck was always "on scene" and had practiced every aspect of firefighting, I knew the volunteer Boy Scouts didn't fight interior attack or climb ladders to the roofs of two- and three-story burning buildings armed with axes to punch-out ventilation holes. No matter the situation, I always knew he was relatively "safe."

But there he stood in the kitchen, just back from a call,

with snowflakes still scattered on his hair, his heavy winter coat making him seem . . . bigger. He placed the permission slip on the table in front of me.

"Please sign it, Mom. The guys think I have enough votes to get in."

"I'm sure you have enough votes to get in, hon," I answered, "and that's what worries me. You could get hurt—or worse."

Chuck removed his coat, sat on the chair closest to me, and looked me in the eyes. "I have more training than a lot of the guys who are already members. The purpose of the training is to allow us to do a dangerous job while keeping ourselves safe."

"If anything ever happened to you . . ."—I paused at the thought—". . . I'd never forgive myself for signing that paper." Surely he could understand my sense of responsibility. I was, after all, the very same mother who once ran through an indoor football-field-length-maze-of-stores-flea-market to find him after his father "lost" him, even as the building was being evacuated for a bomb threat.

"Mom," Chuck said.

I wondered when his voice got so low.

"You've given up a lot to be able to teach us at home," Chuck continued. "And if somehow I forgot most of it, there would always be one thing I remember. You've always told us that the key to a contented life is to 'do what you love.' I've found what I love, Mom."

That little boy with a cape around his neck disappeared. A man sat in front of me, a newly formed man who knew what he wanted and who wasn't going to wait another year in order to pursue it. "Get a pen, please," I said quietly, humbled to witness the fruit of years of hoping, dreaming, and working, believing that my children's education ran so much deeper than reading, writing, and arithmetic.

Six years later, Chuck's life has taken many twists and turns, but he remains habitually late for appointed visits and dinners because someone is trapped in a wrecked automobile or because a chimney fire threatens everything someone owns. He recently informed me that volunteering in the work he loves has caused him to test positive for exposure to tuberculosis, the effects of which remain to be seen. Today, with new respect, people proudly point and call my son a fireman. But because I'll never forget the days before he swapped his make-believe cape for that authentic rescue gear, in my heart he'll remain Superman.

The Maze

Jamie Miller

I WAS ALWAYS LOOKING for adventure during the summer, and a human maze seemed like the perfect place to take my two young sons. It was a hot August day many years ago when we set out for the amusement park that contained this giant outdoor maze. There were several miles of paths to wander before you found your way out. The paths were lined on both sides with ten-foot-high walls to prevent you from seeing anything except what lay directly in front of you. Some people were able to get through the maze in fifteen minutes, and some got stuck in there for more than an hour. I thought it would be an adventure for my two rambunctious boys, Ian, age eight, and Alex, age four.

At three or four strategic points throughout the maze, there were stairs leading to higher ground—lookout platforms, of sorts—for frustrated or unpretentious souls who would surrender to "cheating" occasionally to get their bearings and find the best path through the winding maze. There were also little clusters of parents perched atop these platforms—some watching the process with intrigue and enthusiasm, others shouting directions to their children to help them through and speed up the journey.

As I made my way among these klatches of parents and observed the scene below, I saw all kinds of children. There were kids who were running and laughing, enjoying every minute of the experience—wanting to stay until the park closed and not concerned in the slightest about whether they ever found their way out. They were there for the ride, living in the present, not too worried about succeeding, and oblivious to the time or finish line. My son, Alex, started out in this group.

Then there were the children who were very deliberate about the process. They were analytical and scientific, using their logic to find the best solution to the puzzle. Like little mice sniffing their way to the cheese, they carefully plodded their way along, looking in all directions, counting on all five senses to find their way out.

Some children seemed to have a sixth sense about finding the right path. They were the "naturals"—the ones who needed very little coaching because their instincts seemed to lead them in the right direction. My older son, Ian, fit this category, and it wasn't long before Alex recognized his brother's ability and began to follow Ian at every turn, trusting implicitly that he would lead them both home.

There were other types of children, too. There were those

whose parents didn't seem to be around to shout directions at them and who were left to figure things out for themselves whether they liked it or not. There were children who were reckless. They darted from path to path without regard for anyone or anything around them. They seemed distracted, confused, and frustrated by the complicated course and anxious to get the whole thing over with. This wasn't their idea of fun, and they were looking for the easiest shortcut out of there.

As I watched, it was suddenly clear to me that life, like the maze, is confusing at times for children and some are better-equipped than others to deal with the detours, the sudden changes in direction, and the opportunities at the end of the road. Some will move full steam ahead, confident of their destination, and others will dawdle along the winding road at a much slower rate. Some need lots of help along the way, and others will be successful by just following their noses.

Deep in thought, I had lost track of the time, but I was very aware of one thing: It was hot! The 105-degree heat was beating down on all of us, and I could see its effect on Alex especially, as his chubby little legs tried to keep up with his big brother's energetic stride. About twenty minutes had passed when, suddenly, Alex was down. He simply collapsed, too sweaty and exhausted to keep up and too frustrated to even care about finding his way out of there. He was giving up the race, and the minute I heard his cries, I ran to the rescue.

"Mommy, I hate this!" he sobbed. "Let's go home!"

So that was that. My idea of adventure had proven to be a mild form of torture for one son. Ian, on the other hand, went on to complete the course within a few minutes and came out the exit all smiles and a big, "Yes! Can we do it again?"

A large lemonade later, Alex was himself again but ready to get outta there, and Ian was overruled, two to one. The minute I pulled out of the parking lot, both boys fell fast asleep in the backseat and I drove in silence, pondering the experience. These two boys, whose life experiences had been so similar thus far, were in fact very different. Their approach to life, their unique personalities, their attitudes, the way they tackled problems, their strengths, their weaknesses—almost everything about them was different. It was those differences, I realized, that made them so precious to me. I loved Ian's zest for life and his confidence just as I adored Alex's sweetness and vulnerability.

But beyond that, I thought about the experience of standing on higher ground as a parent—being able to look down and see where each road would take my sons, which paths would lead to roadblocks, and which would lead to success. I thought how much easier it would be if the adventure of life was that clearly visible, that clearly marked, and that my perspective could be as unclouded in raising these two boys. If only I could oversee the whole process, shouting hints along the way—"Watch out! . . . look what's coming! . . . go that way"—pointing out warning signs to help them avoid the major ditches and detours that could cause serious delays or breakdowns.

But just as soon as I had whispered the being-in-control-of-their-journey wish to myself, I knew the foolishness of my desire. True, I would be there to give direction as they grew up. I would try to guide their decisions, teach them the important things in life, and be there to pick them up when they fell and hurt themselves.

But even at their young age, I had known times when my carefully mapped-out plans didn't get us where I thought we should be. I had already negotiated unexpected curves on this parenthood road and been jolted around by unforeseen potholes that left me wondering why someone hadn't fixed the darn road. I had exceeded the speed limit a time or two, expecting them to meet *my* goals sooner than they were ready, and had plodded lazily through other stretches, leaving them restless and unchallenged.

I had a lot of years ahead with my boys, and I knew I had a lot to learn. I would *try* . . . no doubt about that! But on my long drive home that day, I realized that much of what these boys would become in life was simply out of my hands, and that was for a reason. They would forge their own path in their own way on their own schedule. For a good stretch of their journey—through the ups and downs, successes and failures, the joys and heartaches—I was simply privileged to be along for the ride. And I was looking forward to the high adventure.

The Summer I Almost Lost My Golf Partner

Bob Dreizler

ONLY A GOLFER COULD believe that a visit to a driving range would become a sentimental experience, but that's what happened last night. When my fourteen-year-old son picked the last ball from the bucket and crushed one straight and long, I knew I'd be playing for another summer with my favorite golf partner.

Last night Ross was his old happy self again. The cheerful kid I watched grow up was back, temporarily replacing the often-sullen teenage boy he'd become during the last six months.

I've read several books about teenage boys and talked to dozens of parents who have lived through this phase. I know this is normal, even healthy behavior. Fathers and sons are supposed to have an ego separation after years of ego bonding. But knowing that doesn't make life much easier during those times when you feel like your long-time golfing buddy would just as soon his father be a three wood shot away from him.

Ross' interests had changed since last summer. Instead of spending hours perfecting his chip shot in the backyard, he prefers to polish his skateboard moves or play his shiny red drum set in the basement.

When Ross chose not to sign up for Babe Ruth baseball this spring, I was disappointed. I knew I'd dearly miss spending warm afternoons sitting in the stands, watching Ross hustle around the bases or make a sharp play at second base.

Skateboarding was more appealing and not structured like baseball. He could skate with his pals when he wanted, for as long as he wanted. This type of spontaneity was more in harmony with his free-spirited nature.

I accepted my loss of baseball well, I thought, but soon I started to worry that golf would be next. Every summer Wednesday since he was seven, Ross played Little Linkers or Junior Golf at Haggin Oaks. He'd outgrown his clubs, so I asked if he wanted a new set for Christmas. No, he wanted a set of drums. When his birthday came, I offered again, but he chose a new skateboard instead.

Being a "skater dude," he adopted the uniform and temperament of his peers. I accepted the oversize pants and his olive wool cap, but his accompanying scowl and his abrupt answers to my friendly questions really bothered me.

In February, he finally got to play eighteen holes at the beautiful Bodega Bay course that I promised we'd play when he was good enough. We shot a respectable round and thoroughly enjoyed our day together on the links, but after that he declined all my invitations to "putt around" or "hit some at the range."

When it came time to attend the Junior Golf orientation clinic, he was resistant; there were more important things to do. He had made a commitment to play his first round; after that we would reassess his desire to continue.

At the Saturday orientation meeting, he wore his super-baggy blue jeans, despite heat over 100 degrees, and he refused to cover his shaggy skater haircut with the official golf cap.

Wednesday, checking in for his first round, I felt his discomfort at my presence, so I wished him a good round. Before I left, he said he'd be happy to break 110 due to his four-month layoff.

Driving back to my office, I worried that this could be his last round of golf for a long time. It might be years before I'd play eighteen again with my favorite golfing buddy.

When Ross called I was apprehensive, but as soon as I heard his voice I knew his love for golf had not died. "Hey Dad, guess what?" he exclaimed. "I shot a 102." Despite using clubs that were six inches too short, he played well, enjoyed himself, and even met another skater dude.

A week later he shot a 98, breaking 100 for the first time in his life. After that round we visited one of my regular golfing partners. Vic made him an intermediate set of clubs that should fit him for another year or two. By then he'll be my size, or taller, and he'll need a full-size set.

Driving home Ross expressed his enthusiasm, even suggesting we try out his new sticks that night. So after dinner we went to the course, putted around, practiced our chipping, then split a large bucket at the lighted driving range. We were so absorbed that we didn't arrive home until 10 o'clock, half an hour late.

Over the years, my relationship with my son has weathered many challenges. I've enjoyed watching him become a man and develop his own unique interests, but I've also feared those competing interests might extinguish his love for golf. Or quite frankly, for me.

But that night at the driving range, as we hit golf balls and watched them disappear into the warm night sky, I felt confident that we'd be playing rounds together for a long time.

Like most golfers, I don't like to lose, but there's one golf match I've long been eager for. It's the one when my favorite golf partner, my son Ross, outplays me.

He'll Turn Out Okay If You'll Let Him

Lisa Lehr Dodd

HE WAS MY FIRST child, but I suspected almost from those first tiny kicks that he was not like other babies. He was unusually active. The tiny kicks soon became a relentless commotion that led me to wonder if I was carrying twins, or maybe triplets. I'm fairly tall (over 5'9") and reasonably athletic, but for nine months I simply could not eat enough to meet the metabolic demands of this little boy growing inside me.

Yes, I knew—without benefit of ultrasound—that he was a boy. I felt it, and other people said so. Friends gave me blue things and miniature baseball uniforms at my baby shower. Behind me in line at the grocery store, a woman I'd never seen before would say, "It's a boy." Passing me as I walked in my neighborhood, a total stranger would turn and say, "It's a boy."

From the moment of birth, he was the picture of baby perfection, radiantly healthy and cute. We named him Steven, a name that embodied all my expectations: He would be tall, handsome, athletic, smart, popular, and successful. For his middle name, we chose Charles, after my grandfather, who died nine days before I was born.

As the first days unfolded, I discovered I had what the textbooks called a "high need" baby—difficult and unpredictable. In the course of nurturing him, my ability to burn calories shot off the chart. A week out of the hospital, I'd returned to my pre-pregnancy weight. Four months later, I could wear clothes I hadn't worn comfortably in years. "You're thin as a rail," someone would say—with concern or with envy, I'm not sure. By the time Stevie was a year old, I was the thinnest I'd been since early college days, and I could still eat an entire batch of butterscotch brownies if I felt like it.

As the weeks and months went by, little Stevie seemed to be following my plan—sort of. He was calendar-baby beautiful. "He's going to be a lady-killer," people would say. By the time he walked (at sixteen months), he was just a hair shy of three feet tall. "He's going to be a basketball player," people would say.

But even as I beamed amid all the compliments, it was frighteningly obvious that something about him was not normal. "All babies love to ride in the car," some other mother or grandmother would say. And I would want to cry, because Stevie hated riding in the car. He would scream until he was out of breath, rest awhile, and then scream some more. By the time we got where we were going, I was exhausted. "My baby loves the baby swing," another mom would say. "I can put her in there, wind it up, and do whatever I want for hours." Stevie hated the swing; he hated baths; he hated getting dressed and undressed. It seemed he hated anything someone else chose for him. *Why me, Lord?* I found myself wondering.

Stevie was smart, no doubt about that. He learned speech very early, although he didn't necessarily "speak" early. He would listen, watch, and observe, quietly absorbing everything. When he did decide to talk, it was clear he had been paying attention for a very long time, as he began to amaze everyone with his thoughtful questions, his strong opinions, and his uncompromising arguments. "He's going to be a lawyer," people would say.

When he was two-and-a-half, I got a new vacuum cleaner, and for weeks I painstakingly followed the manual as I learned to convert it from one configuration to another. Once, when I got it out, Stevie took it apart while my back was turned and laid the parts all out on the carpet. "He's going to be an engineer," people would say. At other times, he was going to be a forest ranger, a detective, and a stockbroker. He was loaded with potential, there was no doubt about that.

When he started school, the sporadic reports of trouble began. He tore another child's drawing. He sassed the teacher. He would sit on one of the tricycles, not riding it, and not letting anyone else ride it. He walked around when he was supposed to be sitting at his desk. He said rude and cruel things on the playground. He started a rumor that the janitor was drunk. By about second grade, a pattern emerged: Whatever he was supposed to be doing, he was usually doing something else. "Steven's a very bright and curious boy," people would say, "but . . ."

I'd already planned to stay home with him full-time, indefinitely; now, with a second child to care for and then a third, I parked my plans to start a home business firmly on a back burner. I monitored all of Steven's activities: I made sure he watched only public television and Disney movies, I chose his playmates carefully, and I rarely left him with a baby-sitter. I'd always considered myself a reasonably strict parent; now I teetered perpetually on the razor-thin line between caring and controlling.

For years, I had two conflicting mental pictures of Steven as a young man. At times I would see him as the son of my dreams: suntanned, with sun-bleached hair, his letter sweater slung over his shoulder, surrounded by an admiring group of guys and girls as he said one witty and brilliant thing after another, smiling to reveal the dimple on one cheek.

At other times, a darker, more disturbing picture would replace the bright and hopeful one. I'd see an unkempt young man, angry at the world, a social, academic, and professional failure. When my imagination went really berserk, I'd see myself taking my daughters and moving far away while he was in jail, not telling him where we were, in case he wanted to come back and blame me for his failures.

When Steven entered third grade, I had the option of choosing male teachers for him. Every year, third through sixth grade, I chose a male teacher, and whenever possible, ones who had particular expertise in dealing with learning disabilities and behavioral problems. I read volumes about raising boys and about attention disorders. I attended support group meetings. I fought back tears in the doctor's office and in the principal's office. At times when other parents didn't want their sons and daughters making friends with Steven, the professionals tried to assure me that we were doing all the right things and that he would probably turn out okay.

About the time Steve began high school, he said to me, out of the blue, "I'm not going to get in trouble anymore. When you do things wrong in high school, you get in much bigger trouble. So I'm not going to."

And he kept his word.

Who knows what suddenly clicked in his brain. Perhaps it was the accumulated years of seeing what happens to kids who get into trouble, the influence of all the positive role models I could crowd into his life, the assurance that no ill deed would go unnoticed and uncorrected, the trust of those who believed in his God-given gifts. And, perhaps, in no small part, it was the genuine anguish of a mom watching her beloved only son go down the wrong path. If I had withdrawn emotionally—which at times seemed the far easier choice—I fear all might have been lost.

Now sixteen, Steven is growing up to be his own version of himself. He's tall (over 6'4"), big, and strong, though not particularly athletic. He tends more toward the computer genius; he might, in fact, become an engineer. He's good-looking, clean-cut, with naturally dark hair, and no piercings or tattoos. And he still has one dimple. He's bright and gets good grades when he wants to. Maybe he'll get a scholarship to some top-drawer university, and maybe he won't. He's more quiet than popular, but has a small circle of loyal friends—nice, normal young people. He still argues tirelessly and refuses to budge when he thinks he is right, which is pretty much always. He is still occasionally rude, but we always forgive him because the next minute he'll have us falling out of our chairs laughing at his off-the-wall humor.

As for successful, I'm confident he will attain his own version of success. He says he is going to make a lot of money, drive a great car, and have state-of-the-art television and stereo equipment, and the latest electronic toys. He probably will, but the important thing is that the other, dark, disturbing picture of him has faded almost completely away.

If I could express one thing I wish I'd known then that I know now, it would be this: Raising boys is not for the faint of heart and will sometimes require more of you than you have to give. Yet if you honestly do your best, your son will probably turn out okay—even if it's his own version of "okay."

And that's okay.

I Hope She Says "Yes"

Pamela R. Blaine

MY SON HAD MET the girl of his dreams. This was the big night for Jeremy, a huge milestone in his life—the night he was proposing to his girlfriend. For me, it was a time of sentimental reflection, looking back on his life and my life with him. Where had the years gone? Was it possible he was really a senior in college? I couldn't help but think back on a conversation we'd had when he was just a little boy.

"Mommy, I'm going to marry a beautiful woman," he declared out of the blue one day.

"Oh, you are? Well, tell me, Jeremy-pie, just what does a beautiful woman look like?"

He thought a minute, squeezed his eyes shut like he was conjuring up the picture in his mind, and said, "She has big pretty hair, she wears shiny things, and she smells good."

With that, Jeremy had provided a perfect teaching moment for his mother.

"So tell me," I continued, "what if she has all those things but she's really mean and grumpy?"

Without missing a beat he replied, "Then she wouldn't be pretty anymore." Jeremy had passed the test and we talked a little more about the importance of being beautiful on the inside.

Now Jeremy had found Katie, a wonderful girl he had met at college in Hannibal, Missouri, and she was indeed as beautiful on the inside as on the outside. He drove home from college one night, which was an hour from our house, to pick up the engagement ring he had left with me for safe-keeping. It was the night he'd been planning for weeks, and he only stayed home long enough to tell me his plans for popping the question.

Jeremy had told Katie that he was exchanging the necklace he'd given her for Valentine's Day because it was the wrong one. He told her he'd have the new one for her that night but, of course, instead of pulling out the necklace, he would pull out the ring. He told me he was going to propose down along the Mississippi River where they had first kissed. I could just picture my modern-day Tom Sawyer and his Becky Thatcher out on this cold February night, standing beneath snowflakes falling gently on the water, only their love to keep them warm.

When Jeremy pulled out of the driveway, the last thing I said to him was to be careful not to drive too fast. This was my son—I knew him as well as anyone did, and probably better than his bride-to-be would for many years to come. I knew how excited and eager he was, and how that might affect his good judgment. *Of all times,* I knew he was thinking, *he didn't want to be late picking up his date.*

Not too many minutes passed by when my phone rang. It was Jeremy on his cell phone. "Mom!" he shouted. "I got pulled over for speeding." I breathed a sigh of relief because the call had startled me.

"But listen, Mom," he continued. (He wasn't even giving me a chance to get mad.) "You're not going to believe this, but the patrolman asked me why I was in such a hurry and I told him I was on my way back to college to propose to my girlfriend. I was talking as fast as I could, explaining why I didn't want to be late and then I showed him the ring to prove I was telling the truth. The officer looked at my license and registration and then he asked me where I went to college. After he wrote down some stuff on his pad, he handed me the slip of paper and my heart sank because I knew I didn't have money for a ticket."

"Jeremy! It was the last thing I said to you! How could you get a speeding ticket *tonight?*"

"But, Mom," he continued without hardly taking a breath, "When I looked down, I saw that it was just a warning, and I said, 'Oh, thank you!' and I know he could tell how relieved I was. The officer looked me straight in the eye and said, 'You *will* slow down?' I thanked him over and over again, and said, 'Yes, sir. You better believe I will!'"

And then Jeremy told me the best part of all. He said that as the officer started to walk away, he hesitated and turned back as if he'd forgotten to tell my son something important.

"I got engaged at that college, too," he said with a grin. "I hope she says yes." And he walked back to the patrol car.

Later, I asked Jeremy how Katie responded when he proposed and he said, "She cried." I'm sure the ring looked shiny on her finger, and I'm sure she smelled good, too. I never asked about the big pretty hair thing, but I don't think it mattered much anymore. Jeremy had found a new kind of beauty and a new kind of love.

Overdue

M. J. Kornfeld

MY SON IS GOING away to college next year. Actually in 258 days, but who's counting? This phase of our lives reminds me of the last months of pregnancy; my son is too large to share this body, but the thought of moving him out is scarier still. Like the fear of going into labor, you can't really understand the pain until you're in the middle of it. But I wonder what the pain of separation feels like to the newborn baby, or the aftermath of separation. Is it a harsh and distressing shock to his system? Is that why babies cry so much?

Books are written about the process of childbirth, and classes are offered to help expectant mothers prepare. But where are the classes now? During pregnancy, a mother's hormones guide her body through the miraculous process and then doctors and nurses assist when things don't go exactly right. Now, my hormones are depleted and medical science provides no help for this kind of separation and detachment. There is nothing "natural" about this kind of delivery.

The fullness I feel is just like before he was born; I am not comfortable with him in my house as he attempts to emotionally kick his way out. But I am not sure he can survive on his own, cut from my life blood. It might be premature for him to leave, yet daily he grows larger, and we are both constantly aware that he is getting too big to be inside my safe space. When is the due date? Can I survive the wait? Can he?

Just like the last weeks of pregnancy, I am full of him. And he is impatient with me. It's gone on too long—I'm not meeting his needs any longer, and he doesn't care about mine. He takes more than his share of what I have to offer; he eats too much of the food that must sustain us both. He saps my energy during the day. He stays up late, and his wakefulness and activity disturb my sleep. Before, when he was too big for my body, I suffered from heartburn; now his independence makes my heart ache.

But he is still a boy, a minor, and still in my care. He is only an embryo of a man and, like it or not, we are still attached. He doesn't like the restrictions of his overcrowded space, but he is not preparing to move out, either. With no idea about what lies ahead in the hard, cold world—any more than he had the day his body dictated his birth—he is afraid. He won't talk about it, so I know he is afraid. Like the calm before the storm—the days he lay quiet and motionless in my womb just before his birth—there is part of him that wants to cocoon, to remain in the protectiveness of my home.

It's constraining, but still there is nourishment and warmth, and somehow it is better than the unknown.

When I was carrying my son, there were times I needed to lie down and rest, my body sore from bearing the heavy burden of two people on my feet alone. Inevitably, when I would try to relax, he would start his prenatal calisthenics—just as he does now, late at night—rattling drawers and turning on lights, working on projects long after I go to bed. I am tired, and I long for peace and quiet.

When my son was part of me, I knew how to help him. I knew what his growing body needed, and I took in all the right vitamins and proper nourishment to help him develop normally. The formula for growth and development is more complicated and less exact now, and I think I am failing him. He has grown too big. He resists the invisible cord that ties us. He is out there alone, like a spaceman tethered to a spaceship, with one small life support still keeping him from the oblivion of space. Although he yanks and tugs on that line, I know in my heart that he is not looking forward to the day the cord is finally cut.

So when does he leave? 258 days until his due date. My due date. It's like elephant gestation, as the years go by and I grow heavier and heavier with child—with a child waiting to be a man. I know I must create enough space for him to make his own way, to find out who he is. And when he finally does, like it or not, he will likely find that a good part of him resembles the mother who was always there, the mother who is now and always will be within him.

Room with a View

Penny Warner

HIS BAGS ARE PACKED. His stuff is boxed. He's moving out.

After 19½ blissful years of *Star Wars,* Disneyland, McDonald's hamburgers, and silly jokes, my son has decided it's time to find a room with a view of his own. He and his childhood friends—Craig, the enterprising one, Brian, the argumentative one, and Chad, the capricious one—are moving into an apartment together.

Today is moving day. My son's bedroom is literally covered with fully packed boxes. He's borrowing a mattress from the next-door neighbors. He's taking our old living room couch, our old reclining chair, and our old kitchen table. I suggested he take the old dog, too, but he reminded me of the apartment's "no pets" policy.

Last week, while he was out scrounging at the garage sales and flea markets for pots and pans, I sneaked into his room to check the status of packing. I found my favorite Italian cookbook tucked away in one of his half-filled boxes. I pulled it out and made a mental note to buy him some of his own.

Will he really be able to manage without me? I guess so. He's been independent since the day he was born. Knew how to throw together a mean bowl of cereal before he could walk. Whipped up a Mother's Day breakfast in bed that would make Julia Child cry. Last week he fed his buddies spaghetti with leftovers. I guess he won't starve.

On top of one of the boxes was a clipboard with a list titled "Stuff I Will Need." After reading it over, I feel like he's packing for camp or heading for some wonderful vacation spot instead of a new home. "Guitars, footballs, CDs, books, walkie-talkie, Nintendo, video camera, VCR, snowboard, BBQ, dumbells and weights, golf clubs."

Half the stuff he doesn't even own. I guess he's planning to "borrow" a few things from us, just until he gets on his feet. Sounds like he's going to have a wonderful time. The perfect pad for four young men, working their way through college on pizza dough and tips.

In another box I found a brochure for the apartment complex. It's first class (wonder how they qualified?), only three miles away (too far), and huge (a little bigger than his bedroom). It's got a pool, spa, racquetball court, workout facilities, laundry room, and members of the opposite sex. What more could he want?

Underneath the brochure was last year's phone book.

Who's he going to call—his mother? Not likely, not too often. He's got his new phone number already, and I know the number by heart. I might have it tattooed on my ankle.

There's another box full of odds and ends. A flashlight. A tool kit. Some toys and trinkets from his childhood. All of his toiletries. Does he really need all this stuff? I remember when he could have survived on just a toothbrush and his stuffed Sylvester.

I'm not going to get all weepy and sentimental. I knew this day was coming. His lifestyle isn't the same as ours anymore. He stays out late. He sleeps in late. He's rarely home for dinner. He has his own life.

Living on his own will be good for him. He'll learn real-life things we could never teach him in the shelter of home. Like why you need to pay your bills on time. Like what happens when you party too much and have to go to class the next day. Like what you do when you've spent all your grocery money on guitar amps and have to eat mayonnaise and saltine crackers for dinner.

This is something he wants to do. Even though we've given him free room and board, cooked for him, cleaned for him, bought him great toys and cool clothes, and offered him security and affection, he's ready to go it alone.

I keep telling myself it would have happened in a few months anyway, when he transfers to a four-year college. It's just happening a little sooner than I expected.

It's not like I'll never see him again. I'm sure he'll be over to do his laundry, eat a decent meal, or borrow some extra cash when he runs out of pizza tips and needs to pay the electric bill. Besides, maybe he'll get tired of living with a bunch of guys who don't clean up after him, who don't let him watch his favorite TV shows, who don't know he likes popovers for breakfast on Saturdays and foot massages when he gets his teeth pulled and his papers typed at midnight when they're due the next morning. Maybe he'll realize he's made a big mistake.

But of course, that's just not going to happen, is it? I have to accept the inevitable. He's moving out. I have only one thing to say to him before he does.

Don't go.